C0-DVG-374

THE FATE OF MEDIEVAL ART IN THE RENAISSANCE AND REFORMATION

FROM THE COLLECTION OF

Barbara H. Strong

DONATED BY

Ellen C. Gorelick

Tulare Historical Museum
Executive Director-Chief Curator
Emerita

DISCARDED

DISCARDED

HARPER TORCHBOOKS

★

THE CENTRAL GABLE AT WELLS.

THE FATE OF MEDIEVAL ART IN THE RENAISSANCE AND REFORMATION

Part II of
ART AND THE REFORMATION

G. G. COULTON

HARPER TORCHBOOKS

HARPER & BROTHERS, PUBLISHERS
New York

COLLEGE OF THE SEQUOIAS
LIBRARY

To M. R. C.

THE FATE OF MEDIEVAL ART
IN THE RENAISSANCE AND REFORMATION

Part II of *Art and the Reformation*

Art and the Reformation first published by Blackwell, Oxford, 1928
Cambridge University Press edition published 1953

All rights reserved

Reprinted by arrangement with Cambridge University Press

Printed in the United States of America

First HARPER TORCHBOOK edition published 1958

Library of Congress catalog card number: 58-5214

CONTENTS

APPENDIXES

LIST OF ILLUSTRATIONS

PLATES

xi

AUTHORITIES

This list is not in any sense exhaustive, nor is it a bibliography. It is compiled merely for facilitating reference to books which are quoted, but not fully described in the footnotes.

Adderbury " Rectoria "—Oxfordshire Record Soc. vol. VIII, 1926, edited by T. F. Hobson.

A. L. K. G.—*Archiv f. Litt.—u. Kirchengesch. d. Mittelalters.* ed. Denifle & Ehrle, 1885– .

Aube—*Mémoires de la Société académique du département de l'Aube.* Troyes, v.d.

Baldwin Brown—G. Baldwin Brown, *Arts in Early England,* 1903.

Brutails—J. A. Brutails, *Deux chantiers bordelais* (1486–1521) (Extrait du *Moyen Âge* 1899–1901).

Burbure—*Notice sur les auteurs de l'ancien jubé à Bourbourg,* par Léon de Burbure. Lille 1864 (Extrait du *Bulletin du Comité flamand de France,* tome III.).

Cennino—*The Book of the Art of Cennino Cennini,* Christina H. I. Herringham, 1899.

Chapman *Sacrist Rolls*—F. R. Chapman. *Sacrist Rolls of Ely.* Privately printed, 1907.

Cooke-Baker—Brit. Mus. MS. Add. 23,198, probably dating from about 1480, printed by M. Cooke in *History and Articles of Masonry,* 1861.

Crouch—Joseph Crouch, *Puritanism and Art,* 1910.

Cunningham—*Notes on the Organisation of the Mason's Craft in England,* by W. Cunningham, F.B.A. (Pub. Brit. Acad. vol. VI.).

Dejob—Ch. Dejob, *De l'influence du Concile de Trente sur la littérature et les beaux-arts chez les peuples catholiques.*

Didron. *Annales.*—A. N. Didron, *Annales archéologiques.* Paris, 1844.

Didron. *Icon.*—A. N. Didron, *Christian Iconography*, E. H. J. Millington (Bohn's Libraries, 1886).

Edelmaier—*Das Kloster Schönau*, by R. Edelmaier, Heidelberg, 1915.

Gould—R. F. Gould, *History of Freemasonry*, 1883.

Halliwell—J. O. Halliwell, *Early Hist. of Freemasonry in England*, 1844.

Heideloff—Carl Heideloff, *Die Bauhütte des Mittelalters in Deutschland*, Nürnberg, 1844.

Hirn—Yrjö Hirn, *The Sacred Shrine*, Macmillan, 1912.

Janner—F. Janner, *Die Bauhütten d. Mittelalters*, Leipzig, 1876.

Jarrett—Bede Jarrett, O.P., *Social Theories of the M. Ages* (Benn, 1926).

Kendon—Frank Kendon, *Mural Paintings in English Churches during the Middle Ages* (John Lane, 1923).

Kirby Muxloe—A. Hamilton Thompson, *The Building Accts. of K. M. Castle*, in *Trans. Leics. Arch. Soc.* vol. XI., p. 193.

K. K.=Werner Sombart, *Krieg und Kapitalismus*, Leipzig, 1913.

Landucci—*A Florentine Diary*, by Luca Landucci, tr. A. D. Jervis, 1927.

Lefèvre-Pontalis—*Répertoire des architectes &c.*, par E. Lefèvre-Pontalis, Caen, 1912.

Lenoir. *Arch. Mon.*—A. Lenoir, *Architecture monastique*, 1852.

Lethaby. *Craftsmen*—W. R. Lethaby, *Westminster Abbey and the King's Craftsmen*, 1906.

Lethaby. *Med. Art*—W. R. Lethaby, *Medieval Art*, 1904.

Lethaby. *Westminster I*—W. R. Lethaby, *Westminster Abbey and the King's Craftsmen*, 1906.

Lethaby. *Westminster II*—W. R. Lethaby, *Westminster Abbey Re-examined*, 1925.

Life in Medieval Europe—G. G. Coulton, *Life in Medieval Europe*, a reprint of the *Medieval Garner* rearranged in separate volumes by the Camb. Univ. Press.

L. K.=Werner Sombart, *Luxus und Kapitalismus*, Leipzig, 1913.

Mâle I—Émile Mâle. *L'art religieux du XIIᵉ siècle en France*, Paris, 1922.

Mâle II—Émile Mâle. *L'art religieux du XIIIe siècle en France,* Paris, 1898.

Mâle III—Émile Mâle. *L'art religieux de la fin du moyen âge en France,* Paris, 1908.

Med. Build. Doc.—A. Hamilton Thompson, *Medieval Building Documents* (Presidential Address, in *Proc. Somerset Arch. Soc.* vol. LXVI., 1920).

Medieval Garner—G. G. Coulton, *A Medieval Garner,* 1908.

Merrifield—*Original Treatises on the Arts of Painting,* by Mrs. Merrifield, 1849.

M. K.=Werner Sombart, *Der Moderne Kapitalismus,* vol. II., pt. ii., Munich and Leipzig, 1919.

Molanus—Joannes Molanus, *De Historia SS. Imaginum et Picturarum,* ed. J. N. Paquot, Louvain, 1721.

Mortet—V. Mortet, *Recueil de textes relatifs à l'hist. de l'architecture, &c.,* 1911.

Müntz—E. Müntz, *Les arts à la cour des papes.* This came out in four instalments; the first three were published in *Bib. des écoles françaises d'Athènes et de Rome,* in 1878, 1879, and 1882 respectively; the last by Leroux in 1898. I quote the volumes by their respective dates.

Quicherat—*Mélanges d'archéologie et d'histoire,* par Jules Quicherat. Série II, 1886.

Renan and Leclerc—*Discours sur l'état des lettres. . . . Discours sur l'état des beaux-arts . . . au 14e siècle* (reprinted from *Hist. litt. de la France,* second ed. 1865).

Riley—H. T. Riley, *Memorials of London, &c.,* 1868.

Schlosser, Beiträge—Julius v. Schlosser, *Beiträge zur Kunstgeschichte, u.s.w.,* in *Sitzungsberichte d. phil. hist. Classe d. K. Akad. in Wien,* vol. 123, 1891.

Schlosser, Quellenbuch—J. v. Schlosser, *Quellenbuch z. Kunstgeschichte, u.s.w.,* Vienna, Graeser, 1896.

Schnaase—K. J. F. Schnaase, *Gesch. d. bild. Künste,* 1843– .

Social Life in Britain—G. G. Coulton, *Social Life in Britain from the Conquest to the Reformation,* Camb. Univ. Press, 1918.

Test Eborac.=*Testamenta Eboracensia,* Surtees. Soc., 1836–69.

Westlake, *Last Days*—H. F. Westlake, *Westminster Abbey, the Last Days of the Monastery*, 1921.

Willis and Clark—R. Willis and J. W. Clark, *Architectural History of the University of Cambridge*, 1886.

Wulf—M. de Wulf, *Philosophy and Civilization in the Middle Ages* (1922).

ADDENDA

Page 337: Professor Baldwin Brown writes: "The story is in itself perfectly true and attested by contemporary records; but it was played not at Florence but at Siena, and the painter was the Sienese Duccio, the picture his great altarpiece for the Duomo."

Page 485, line 3: Honorius's actual words are here accidentally omitted: they run: "Almost all [of the various classes of artificers] are damned; for whatsoever they do, they do with the greatest fraud" (Migne, *P.L.*, vol. 172, col. 1148, c).

G. G. C.

CHAPTER XVI

ART AND RELIGION

THE thirteenth century achieved an equilibrium of art and religion which, though neither so complete nor so stable as it is often represented, was yet very real. Through the Dark Ages, art had been preserved mainly in the cloister, by monastic money and even sometimes by monastic hands. In many cases, also, it had been penetrated by a genuine and deep devotional spirit. Though Tuotilo of St. Gall is acknowledged now to be partly legendary—for our records date from a century later than his actual day, and Ekkehard, who describes him at length, is unquestionably so inaccurate as to confuse between different generations at that monastery— yet at least his story is in all respects *ben trovato*, and an unregenerate modern historian of art might echo those contemporary words : " Curses on the man who made so fine a fellow as this into a monk ! " The legend of his work at Metz rests also upon real facts ; monks did indeed, here and there, wander forth from their abbeys to work for churches outside. Some, again, like that Roger of Helmershausen, who called himself Theophilus, collected small groups of pupils, and jotted down practical notes for their use. But a careful analysis of the facts indicates that all this tradition was monastic mainly in the sense that it was sheltered within the monastic precincts. Nearly all these practical recipes of the Middle Ages can be traced back to Greek or Egyptian paganism. The two arts which monks themselves seem most to have practised are metal-work and illumination. Neither of these is distinctly Christian in its origin or in its general character ; they are Christianized, if at

all, only by the addition of certain details which are in
no way essential to the general artistic effect.[1] We may
see this in the Gloucester candlestick at the Victoria and
Albert Museum ; or, still better, in the thirteenth
century huge bronze candelabrum of Milan Cathedral.
The central boss, occupying perhaps one-fiftieth of the
whole mass, contains four groups from the Adoration of
the Magi ; but most of the rest is undenominational ;
with very little change of detail, and none of general
effect, the candelabrum might light a temple of Buddha
or of Vishnu. Moreover, even the details in our churches
were not always distinctively Christian. We have seen
how ostrich-eggs were borrowed from mosques ; and the
baldacchino of Roman churches was originally, as its name
tells us, simply a hanging of those brocades for which
Baldak, or Bagdad, has always been famous. It is probable that the great statue of Peter in his own church
at Rome, whose toes have been kissed away by generations of worshippers, was originally a Jupiter.

For early Christianity had been strongly puritan in
the matter of art ; and, when at last it adopted painting
and sculpture, it accepted pre-existing pagan traditions
for its basis. Remi de Gourmont, though he hated and
despised Protestantism, was driven to energetic protest
against the sentimental figments of Huysmans on the
subject of medieval art. "The worship of saints
and of sanctified deities," he writes, "begat churches.
The Catholic churches, like the temples of ancient
Egypt, are tombs ; they were not built in honour
of God alone ; their pretext was almost always to
shelter the corpse of a saint or a miracle-worker, the

[1] The pre-Christian tribes of Europe had excelled in elaborate metal-
work ; and their laws show clearly how great a value was attached to
metal-workers in comparison with other craftsmen. In almost every
code a higher fine must be paid in redemption for killing a goldsmith
than for any other. "The goldsmith has almost everywhere the highest
'weregeld.' From the 30 to 50 *solidi* [gold pieces] which are prescribed
by the Salic and Alamannic Laws, it rises among the Burgundians to 100,
or even 150." (J. v. Schlosser, *Beiträge*, p. 175.)

simulacrum of some traditional deity scarcely even
re-baptized by an innocent piety. . . . [Huysmans] tries
to prove that there is, or rather that there has been, a
Catholic, symbolic and mystic art, far above profane
art, especially in expression. . . . There is a Catholic
art ; there is no such thing as Christian art. Evangelical
Christianity is essentially opposed to all representations
of sensible beauty, whether imitated from the human
body or from the rest of nature. . . . Whenever Christianity, through its monks or its revolutionaries, has
tried to force itself to closer conformity with apostolic
teaching, it was compelled to reject all that there was in
the Roman religion of paganism in beauty, and consequently of sensualism. There is no Christian art ; it is
a contradiction in terms. . . . The pagan origin of the
symbolism of the catacombs is certain ; it was mythology
which supplied the decorative elements to the tombs of
the first martyrs. . . . The martyrs who refused incense
to idols would have been very surprised if they had been
told that the censer would become a pious article of
furniture."[1] The best churchmen of the Middle Ages, as
we shall see, made no attempt to confuse art with religion.
   Yet in practice the two were inextricably intermingled, when once the Church had committed herself
to the Græco-Roman rather than the Jewish attitude
towards art. "Catholic art . . . is the natural and
logical sequence of pagan art."[2] It refused that complete
breach with the past which the earlier Fathers had aimed
at, and which others again attempted at the Reformation. The Church needed churches, and for them she
needed artists ; thenceforward there was continual
interaction. The ubiquitous character of the medieval
Church can scarcely be exaggerated. In England, which
represents about the average, there was more than one
parish church to every hundred families, without counting chapels or wayside shrines. The proportion was even

[1] *La Culture des Idées,* ed. du *Mercure de France,* 1916, pp. 139–155.
[2] Ibid., p. 140.

greater in the towns than in the villages. Norwich had about 50 churches when its total population was more probably 8,000 than 12,000 souls, Lincoln had 49, York 41.[1] And these buildings entered not merely into religious life but into men's daily affairs. As the priest claimed authority over all baptized folk from the cradle to the grave and in almost every act of their lives, so the consecrated building was more their home than it is nowadays, even in modern Roman Catholic countries. A modern French church is sometimes placarded with notices asking the worshippers, among other things, not to bring packages into the sacred building ; but in Italy the peasant woman still brings in her market-basket, and sets it down under the pulpit if she stops to listen to a sermon. Lawsuits and university disputations and degree-ceremonies were regularly carried on in medieval churches. This had its irreverent side ; litigation and theatrical performances were often forbidden, though not with complete success. At Strassburg, one of the Burgomaster's most regular places and times for business was his pew in the cathedral during Mass. Saintliest ecclesiastics did not shrink from doing business during the sacred office ; St. Hugh of Lincoln, in the chapel of Château-Gaillard, held an animated dispute with Richard I, before he passed on to the altar and "attended to naught else but the divine service."[2] Of Henry II, who was quite an average God-fearing man as medieval kings went, Giraldus tells us that "either forgetting his own sacramental unction as king, or putting it out of his mind, he would scarce lend to God's worship just the time of consecration in the Mass ; and even during that time (perchance by reason of his royal cares and the heavy business of the State), he was more busy with his councillors, and with talk, than with devotion to the sacrament."[3] "When he went intoh is chapel,"

[1] Baldwin Brown, p. 119.
[2] Magna Vita S. Hugonis, R.S., p. 251.
[3] Giraldus Cambrensis, De Instructione Principum, 1846, p. 72.

says another contemporary, " he would spend the time in whispering and scribbling pictures."[1] The chronicler of Battle Abbey tells us how the Abbot of Westminster, a few days after Henry II's coronation, was so anxious to get confirmation of a charter of privileges for his abbey, that he came to the king during Mass and got the king to read and approve it ; the king then sent for the chancellor and got it sealed ; then came up the Bishop of Chichester and protested against the charter. All this certainly took place during Mass, and apparently almost at the foot of the altar.[2]

But there was a better side to all this, and we must beware of judging it from a narrowly modern point of view ; it was partly childish, but it was also in great part childlike. The people felt that this was their own building, their one natural meeting-place outside the family fireside. We must not think of it as a place of complete equality ; the squire had a right of sitting apart in the chancel with the clergy, and Chaucer, among others, shows us how neighbours struggled for precedence in accordance with their competing social claims.[3] Yet the Church had kept a good deal of ancient Christian democratic tradition ; and, among the large majority who acquiesced more or less completely in her authority, the sacred building was a real home ; so that they nestled within its walls with some true portion of that spirit of adoption whereby we cry *Abba, Father*, the Spirit itself bearing witness with our spirit that we are the children of God. It was bound up with a spirit of local patriotism, narrow but intense ; the inhabitant even of the next village or town is spoken of in market-regulations as a " foreigner " ; when different villages repair on solemn festivals to the nearest cathedral, each with the banner of its own local saint, there are fierce struggles for precedence, often ending in bloodshed and sometimes in

[1] Radulphus Niger (ed. Anstruther), p. 169.
[2] *Chron. de Bello*, 1846, p. 72.
[3] *Cant. Tales*, B, 3091 ; cf. *The Medieval Village*, pp. 283 ff.

death."[1] On the other hand, within the parish there was a strong sense of social solidarity. The mere sight of men's faces and sound of voices in peaceful surroundings, and in homage to a single ideal, however vaguely understood, exercises a progressive humanizing influence. However the hierarchy was feudalized, there was at bottom the theory of the equality of all souls; and this was realized to some extent in the community of worship and of the Sacraments. There is equal religious and artistic significance in that story, dear to Burne-Jones and his friends, of the Merciful Knight who spared his enemy and for whom, next time he knelt before the crucifix, the Christ-figure bent down from that cross to embrace him. Provided that men thought at all (a proviso as necessary for the estimate of medieval as of modern society) there was the daily thought of Christ suffering and redeeming, and, still more, of the Virgin Mary as mediator, side by side with the strict Judge who sits aloft over the chancel arch, and shows five bleeding wounds that cry for vengeance like Abel's. The parish church, then, was where faces and voices met; a sort of spiritual (and sometimes, even material) market-place. Under stress of great sorrow, it was still more; refreshing, uplifting, and affording the one hope there was for the dead.

In many ways, therefore, churchman and artist were natural allies, and art was kept in natural touch both with the religious idealist up above and with popular ideas down below. Probably the craftsman's personal preference would generally have been for a completer independence; but the Church paid him and the Church did much to

[1] E.g. Grosseteste, *Epistolæ*, R.S., p. 75. The author of an admirable recent study of a single Burgundian village writes: " Formerly, interparochial hatred was general; villages hated and insulted each other; on the feast of the patron saint something was lacking to the full festival if there was no fight among the young folk. . . . When, about 1840, the first Arbigny girl married an Uchizy man, there was a sort of riot in the parish on the wedding-day. (Ch. Dard, *Uchizy en Mâconnais*, Mâcon, 1926. p. 144.)

call the tune, if not directly, at least indirectly, in the sense that the building must be constructed to serve ecclesiastical purposes and traditions, even when the funds were raised by mere layfolk. Therefore, although it is likely that the hierarchy did little more to shape art directly than to shape vernacular literature—and in that field its influence can be calculated with some approach to exactitude—yet the indirect influence of the Church was immense. The thesis of the communal origin of the ballad is often defended on the ground that the requirements of ballad poetry were practically dictated by communal conditions ; [1] and in that same sense we may emphasize the ecclesiastical character of medieval art.

To claim more for it than this would seem inconsistent with historical facts. The theory of a direct connexion between art and religion is paradoxical, to say the least, in the face of what we know about society in the thirteenth century, or, again, in the age of Pericles. The generations which produced our greatest cathedrals were those in which we can trace a strong spirit of doubt, both philosophic and popular. University scholars were then condemned for formulating difficulties strikingly similar to the difficulties felt by the majority of thinking people in this twentieth century ; and it would be absurd to suppose, even if we had not explicit evidence to the contrary, that the teachers who were bold enough to provoke these censures were the only men who thought thus in their hearts ; or, again, that this ecclesiastical condemnation did in fact reverse the current of their thoughts. Moreover, there is evidence for widespread popular unbelief also, in cruder forms.[2] So again with the age of Pericles, as no less an authority than Jebb has pointed out.[3] This was the age of perfect Greek art, and also of

[1] E.g. G. L. Kittredge, on pp. 20 ff. of *English and Scottish Popular Ballads*, ed. Sargent and Kittredge, (Houghton, Mifflin & Co., 1904.)

[2] Cf. *From St. Francis to Dante*, Chapter XXIV.

[3] *Has Art thriven best in an Age of Faith ?* This rare pamphlet, embodying a lecture given at Glasgow in 1889, seems never to have been reprinted. I summarize it in Appendix 25.

widespread scientific scepticism. Ruskin generalizes from these facts : " The religious passion is nearly always vividest when the art is weakest ; and the technical skill reaches its deliberate splendour only when the ecstasy which gave it birth has passed away for ever." [1] And at another time, in *The Stones of Venice* : " The more I have examined this subject, the more dangerous I have found it to dogmatize respecting the character of the art which is likely, at a given period, to be most useful to the cause of religion. One great fact first meets me. I cannot answer for the experience of others, but I never yet met with a Christian whose heart was thoroughly set upon the world to come, and, so far as human judgment could pronounce, perfect and right before God, who cared about art at all. . . . I have never known a man who seemed altogether right and calm in faith, who seriously cared about art." [2]

It is true that certain forms of religion appeal specially to the artistic temperament ; but so also do certain forms of irreligion. Of Perugino, whose actual pictures would never have suggested this, Vasari tells us that he could never get any notion of God into that hard head of his.[3] Of all present races, it is probable that the most artistic are the Chinese, among whom the educated classes are said to be conspicuous for their lack of religious enthusiasm.

The Middle Ages provide no true exception to this general law in social history. Not only was the medieval Church never mistress of man's artistic emotions, but she never claimed to be, except so far as she asserted a right of censorship over all men's actions, in the interest of her dogmatic traditions. Bishop Baldock of London might, for his own diocese, forbid an artistic crucifix as

---

[1] *The Queen of the Air*, library edition, vol. xix, p. 384.

[2] IV. *St. Mark's*, § 58, ed. vol. x, p. 125.

[3] It is interesting to connect this with what Sacchetti tells us of superstition in Perugia, and the connexion between superstition and infidelity. See Chapter XIV above.

heretical; but I believe that no pre-Renaissance popes ever attempted to regulate art in general, any more than they attempted to revise the notoriously corrupt text of the Vulgate Bible. Charlemagne, it is true, attempted both. His Bible-revision, with the similar work of Roger Bacon and his school, marked the only great forward steps in that field during the last nine centuries of the Middle Ages; next in importance came the work of another Englishman, Stephen Harding. And in art, as we have seen, Charlemagne intervened also, with sound sense though not with enduring success. There were other individuals, as we shall see, who strongly objected to grotesques and obscenities, especially in churches. An inconvenient reformer like Savonarola might persuade people for a moment to make bonfires of lascivious pictures and expensive artistic superfluities; but Savonarola himself became food for the faggot, chiefly because of his determined opposition to the reigning clerical tendencies of his time. When at last popes became seriously interested in art, they were far from sharing Savonarola's attitude towards morals, or Charlemagne's towards image-worship.

The puritanism of great medieval religious reformers is very notable. The remarkable reform of Cluny is often quoted in the contrary direction, but by an anachronism. It is true, Cluny had probably a very large part in that movement which produced Glaber's often-cited " white robe of churches " in the first half of the eleventh century. But the reform itself had begun a century before this; and we need evidence for any real revival of art under Cluniac influence during the first and purest generations. Moreover, the churches of which Glaber speaks were probably what we should consider extremely plain; it is only in the century after his death, roughly from 1070 to 1170, that we have evidence for Cluniac workshops and a whole school of remarkable sculpture and metal work. But by that time there was a good deal of worldliness in the congregation; the Cluniacs as a whole did not even declare definitely for Gregory VII in his quarrel with Henry IV ; and the Abbot of Cluny kept friendly relations with the emperor. Therefore it is obviously impossible to argue from what we know of A.D. 1100, when the Cluniacs were among the wealthiest bodies in the Western world, back to 910, when they had started on a career of evangelical poverty. It follows that, pending the production of entirely new evidence, Cluny cannot be quoted as exemplifying an alliance of pure art with pure religion.

For the next great reformers, the Cistercians, we have abundant evidence of puritanism ; indeed, among the modern orthodox there are not a few who accuse them here of straitlaced Phariseeism. They were anxious above all " to follow, naked, the naked Christ : " from this followed logically their determination " that nothing savouring of pride or superfluity should be left in God's house." [1] The Cistercians, writes Abbé Vacandard, " vowed to remove from their lowly chapels everything which might flatter curious eyes and charm weak souls. They banished painting and carving, as vain things that were good for worldly folk. The same prohibition extended to fine tissues and precious metals ; the very crosses might not be plated with silver or copper, they were to be of wood." [2] This dates from their very beginning ; it is expressed in St. Stephen Harding's " Charter of Charity," which is the constitutional foundation-stone of the Order.

And these Cistercians, zealous for reform, did not hesitate to plead openly and definitely here against the Cluniacs, whom they rightly recognized as representatives, in that day, less of Benedictine strictness than of monastic relaxation. St.-Bernard, in his letter to Guillaume de St.-Thierry, wrote with a satirical emphasis which would not have been fully endorsed by cultured

---

[1] Migne, P.L., vol. 185, col. 1011 ; cf. *Five Cent. of Religion*, vol. i, p. 278.

[2] *Vie de St.-Bernard*, 2nd ed., vol. i, p. 101.

Anglican puritans like Milton and Selden ; and yet St. Bernard, like those men, had been brought up in the literary tradition of the Roman classics, as they were taught in his own day.[1] The size and elaborate orna- mentation of the Cluniac churches, says the saint, seem distinctive less of Christian worship than of Jewish rites. All this gilding and these sensuous attractions, are they meant to secure " the admiration of fools, or the offerings of simple folk ? " " To speak plainly, doth the root of this lie in covetousness, which is idolatry ? and do we seek not [spiritual] profit, but a gift " ? according to the worldly law which often renders ostentation a successful bait for further endowments. " Men's eyes are feasted with relics cased in gold, and their purse-strings are loosed." The net result is, that " the Church is resplen- dent in her walls, beggarly in her poor ; she clothes her stones in gold and leaves her sons naked ; the rich man's eye is fed at the expense of the indigent." He is specially severe upon the magnificent hanging chandelier of bronze which was one of the greatest ornaments of Cluny. The very floors, again, are pictured, so that men spit in the face of an angel. For simple and uneducated folk, St. Bernard does permit some of these attractions ; they may need artificial stimulus ; but for his fellow-religious he is inexorable. The grotesques which adorn the Cluniac cloisters do but distract the truly pious mind ; " we are tempted to spend the whole day in wondering at these things, rather than in meditating on the law of God." It will be noted that Bernard, like Charlemagne, emphasizes not any hidden meaning supposed to underlie these grotesques, but their want of meaning. Schnaase writes very truly : " We possess a series of passages, from the twelfth century to the fifteenth, in which ecclesiastical writers mention animal representations, sometimes with sharp blame, as contrary to the dignity of a sanctuary, and sometimes with praise for their vivid execution, but never with the slightest reference to their symbolical

[1] See Appendix 26 for fuller text of this and similar utterances.

character, though this could not have passed unnoticed if
symbolism had been usual here. Therefore these fully-
instructed men either did not assume any such meaning,
or held it to be so little disseminated as to require no
refutation." [1] I have already noted how St. Bernard,
speaking bitterly of the wastefulness of such objects, gives
no hint of monks' time or energies squandered on these

artistic treasures, but of money
wasted which might have gone to
feed and clothe the destitute.
Moreover, this spirit of St. Stephen
Harding and St. Bernard lived on
among many Cistercians of the next
generation. It comes out very
strongly in the *Dialogue between a
Cluniac and a Cistercian,* of about
1180. There, the Cluniac is
shocked at St. Bernard's satire : " I
have read it, and marvelled how he
could so reprove those insignia of
our religious devotion (whereby we
honour God), as to hold us up to
scorn." To which the Cistercian
answers : " Did those unknown
authors of your Order imagine

FROM FUNERAL BRASS OF
ABBOT DELAMERE AT
ST. ALBANS (HERTS).

that, at the Last Day, Christ
would thus say (among other things)
to the Elect : ' *Come, ye blessed of
My Father* [2] *for ye have made a golden chalice in My
honour, and a chasuble with golden fringes ;* ' and that He
would make some contrary speech to the damned ? "

Petrus Cantor, the famous precentor of Notre-Dame-

[1] Vol. ii, pt. 1, p. 376 ; see the whole discussion from p. 369 onwards.
[2] Martène, Thes., vol. v, col. 1585. On the verge of the Reformation,
Abbot Tritheim repeated what others had said before him, that magnificent monastic buildings were only too often concomitants of spiritual
decay (*Opp. Pia*, p. 884). For further evidence see *Five Cent. of Religion*,
vol. i. For a· very interesting further example of Cistercian puritanism,
about 1230, see Renan and Leclerc, vol. i, p. 71.

de-Paris, wrote at the time when this *Dialogue* was being composed. He also takes the puritan standpoint ; these great monastic buildings are often raised from the proceeds of usury or " the deceitful lies of hireling preachers," and " men sin even in building churches," for these preach rather pride than Christian humility.[1] So thought St. Francis also, insisting that the poverty of the brethren's churches would preach better than words. Thomas of

FROM FUNERAL BRASS OF BISHOPS BURCHARD
AND JOHN AT LÜBECK.

Eccleston tells us how loyal the English friars of the first generation had been to that ideal. [2] "At Shrewsbury Brother William, the minister, being zealous for poverty, ordered the stone walls in the dormitory to be removed and mud walls put in their stead, which was done by the brethren with admirable meekness and at great cost." And again, " Under Brother Agnellus the brethren had so strict a conscience regarding the building of houses and the possession of pictures that the visitor acted with great severity because of the windows in the chapel at Gloucester ; moreover, he deprived a brother of his hood

[1] *Verb. Abbrev.*, chap. lxxxvi.
[2] *Monumenta Franciscana*, R.S., pp. 18, 29.

because he had decorated a pulpit with pictures, and he inflicted the same penance upon the Guardian of the place because he had permitted the pictures to be painted."

Humbert de Romans (about 1270), criticized severely the architectural indulgences to which by this time even the Cistercians had become accustomed : " There are some, among whom there is such excess in buildings, either in number or in cost or in elaboration of ornament [*curiositatem*], that they surpass even worldly folk." He is indignant also " that there is an excessive costliness in books, and especially in the books of Religious, who ought specially to profess poverty. St. Jerome would have us care not so much for beautiful texts, as for texts carefully corrected." [1] He writes as General of the Dominicans, who had begun in the same spirit of puritanism with the Franciscans, though perhaps with rather less militant directness.[2] And in the fifteenth century, when all Orders of Friars sadly needed recall to their first simplicity, grave warnings were uttered by another Dominican, St. Antonino, Archbishop of Florence.[3] He was a great canon lawyer and a confessor of vast experience ; his knowledge of mankind and his common sense enabled him to get as near as any other man to that reconciliation of usury and religion which had been begun by earlier thinkers, and especially by St. Thomas Aquinas. But, in the matter of art, he agreed with St. Bernard and St. Francis. Taking his text from Gratian, the first book of the *Corpus Juris Canonici*, he wrote : " Note that St. Ambrose saith [Gratian, pars. i., dist. 86, c. 18], ' It is specially proper for the priest to adorn God's temple with suitable honour, in order that God's hall may shine with such ornaments also.' Yet he saith not that we should

---

[1] De la Bigne, *Bib. Max. Patrum*, vol. xxv, pp. 465, 633. It will be noted here again that his objection to these illuminated volumes is not waste of monks' labour, but waste of money : by this time, even the illuminations were mainly done by paid workmen.

[2] E.g. the statutes of 1228, printed by Ehrle and Denifle (*Archiv.*, vol. i, p. 225).

[3] *Summa Major*, pars. iii, tit xii, cap. x, § 2.

make superfluities, pomps, and many vanities of coats of
arms, of paintings, of golden vessels and so forth. . . .
St. Jerome [*ibid*., pars. ii, causa xii, c. 71] in his epistle
to Nepotianus, saith : ' Many folk build walls, and rear
columns for the church ; we see gleaming marbles, and
the roofs are bright with gold ; the altar is adorned with
gems ; yet no care is taken to choose the ministers of
Christ. Let no man here plead against me that the
temple of the Jews was rich ; that it had a golden table,
golden lamps, dishes and cups and covers of beaten gold.
Such things were then approved by God, while the priests
slaughtered beasts for sacrifice—that is, while the people
were as yet carnal, and God's worship was sought in
outward and sensible things ' ; but then Jerome con-
tinueth [1] : ' Yet all these things were preparatory and
figurative, and were written for our correction, upon
whom the ends of the world are come [1 Cor. x. 11].
Now, however, when our Lord, as a poor man, has consecrated the poverty of His own house, let us bear His
cross and look upon delights [2] as dirt.' St. Bernard also
reprehendeth the vain and monstrous pictures of churches,
and the filth and carelessness of sacred things, as of altar-
cloths and so forth." And elsewhere, speaking of architecture and art in general, he writes : [3] " The reprobate
Cain is the first of whom we read that he built a city, and
therefore houses. . . . After the deluge, the tyrant
Nimrod was the first who led others to build the tower
of Babel. . . . Spacious palaces and excessive buildings,
beyond what is convenient, are not pleasing to God ; the
Patriarchs lived in tents." . . . St. Antonino then speaks
of *latomi* and *caementarii*, and continues : " Stone-cutters
are joined with these, whereof some hew stones and bring
them to a rough shape, whence others complete divers
finished works, others carve statues and figures, as marblers
also ; and these cannot make many frauds in their works,

[1] I.e. this parenthesis is Antonino's gloss upon Jerome.
[2] Gratian has *divitias*, not *delicias*.
[3] Ibid., pars. iii, tit. viii, cap. iv, § 8.

for such works are manifest to all men ; yet they can demand an excessive price for their labour ; nevertheless, if experts in art esteem the work at such a price, we must believe them."[1] We have seen how the author of *Dives and Pauper*, himself in all probability a friar, is emphatic as to the non-religious character of a great deal of church-building. St. Bernardino of Siena counts it a sin in artisans to make superfluous and sumptuous curtains, shirts in which the embroidery is worth ten times the material, costly caps or garlands for ladies, or playing-cards.[2] Dean Colet, in his famous Convocation sermon of 1511, complained that the goods of the Church were too often spent on sumptuous edifices.[3]

These quotations may suffice out of a far larger number which might be produced. Art devotees in the Middle Ages were of almost all sorts, but they were seldom or never canonized saints. St.-Eloi, who is frequently quoted, is no real example here ; there is, I believe, no evidence for his having practised art-work from the moment of his conversion onwards. Fra Angelico would be a nearer instance, if we are to choose the best case we can produce from about a thousand years of history. The heroes of the most romantic episodes in medieval art history are not the hierarchy but the lay public. They are not saints, but the better sort of ordinary people ; this will come out more clearly in my next chapter.

But let me here repeat that it is no part of my thesis to deny the intimate connexion between the art of any age and the religion of that age. Many indications of this connexion will be obvious to everybody ; and, quite recently, Emile Mâle and other authors have shown that the pilgrimage-routes did as much as the trade-routes

---

[1] "The parishioners of Totnes in 1488 appointed a committee of 'supervisors' to visit all the bell-towers for miles around, and afterwards built one at Totnes 'according to the best model'."—*Hist. MSS. Comm.* III, 235–346.

[2] *Opera*, ed. de la Haye, vol. i, p. 161 ; cf. iii, 160 (elaborate music offensive to God's ears).

[3] Knight's *Life of Colet.*, 1823, p. 247.

for the spread of new ideas in art, or perhaps even more.[1] It is my aim only to clear this question and to guard against exaggerations. However real and potent and ennobling may be the religious emotion inspired in us by art, or the religious emotions which inspired certain artists in their own day, let us not forget that this does not appeal equally to all men ; and, again, that there are other high religious appeals quite independent of art. We shall best learn, and best enjoy, by taking each on its own merits. And, when either theologian or artist is tempted to complain that something in the atmosphere of his own day frustrates his efforts, will he not then, in proportion as he has the real root of the matter in his soul, hear a voice descending from that which he is aspiring to reach : " What is that to thee ? Follow thou Me."

Yet there was, at certain times and places, what may be called a real Religion of Art. Vasari has told the story of Cimabue and the Borgo Allegri, the Suburb of the Joyful, in words which modern historians dare not endorse as accurate, but which are not beyond the bounds of probability ; the anecdote may be accepted as *ben trovato* so long as we refrain from undue emphasis.[2] " He afterwards painted the Picture of the Virgin, for the Church of Santa Maria Novella. This picture is of larger size than any figure that had been painted down to that time ; and the angels surrounding it made it evident that, although Cimabue still retained the Greek manner, he was nevertheless gradually approaching the mode of outline and general method of modern times. Thus it happened that this work was an object of so much admiration to the people of that day—they having then never seen anything better—that it was carried in solemn procession, with the sound of trumpets and other festal

[1] E.g. *Revue de Paris*, Oct. 15, 1919. " L'Art du Moyen âge et les pèlerinages."

[2] *Lives of the Painters*, ed. Bohn, vol. i, p. 41. As the editor points out, the suburb almost certainly drew its name from the Allegri family.

demonstrations, from the house of Cimabue to the church ; he himself being highly rewarded and honoured for it. It is further reported, and may be read in certain records of old painters, that, whilst Cimabue was painting this picture, in a garden near the Church of San Pietro, King Charles the Elder, of Anjou, passed through Florence, and the authorities of the city, among other marks of respect, conducted him to see the picture of Cimabue. When this work was thus shown to the King, it had not before been seen by any one ; wherefore all the men and women of Florence hastened in great crowds to admire it, making all possible demonstrations of delight. The inhabitants of the neighbourhood, rejoicing in this occurrence, ever afterwards called that place Borgo Allegri ; and this name it has ever since retained, although in process of time it became enclosed within the walls of the city."

But we have a far more remarkable story, upon far better evidence, from about the year 1155. It is told at length by Henry Adams in *Mont St.-Michel and Chartres*. But Adams was a superficial student, and the whole book, in spite of the author's real ability and the interest of his subject, is full of false impressions. Under a style which implies a vast reserve of learning from which the writer is drawing almost at random, he conceals a frequent ignorance of the most important documents ; and, in this particular case, writing apparently at second-hand, he mistakenly applies to Chartres a description which does, indeed, cast a very valuable sidelight on that cathedral, but which in the original source, points in direct and full detail only one corner of Normandy.

For Chartres, we have a brief but valuable record in a single sentence from the pen of a contemporary archbishop of Rouen. In a letter to the Bishop of Amiens, he says : " At Chartres, men began in their humility to drag carts and waggons for the building of the cathedral ; and their humility was even illuminated by miracles."[1]

[1] Mabillon, *An. Bened.*, vol. vi, p. 392.

Next comes a little treatise, written shortly after this, by Haymo, Abbot of St.-Pierre-sur-Dives, in Normandy. He tells us that the movement began at Chartres, but dismisses this in as few words as the archbishop. Then, turning to what he can speak of in his own district, as an eye-witness, he tells a story of extraordinary interest.

From Chartres, he says, this wave of enthusiasm spread over most of the Île-de-France and Normandy, " and many other places." It was part of a sudden religious revival.[1] He begins by describing the religious decay of his own generation—a generation which " had almost forgotten God." " If it had not been for this revival," he says, " Christ would have found no faith and no faithful people left on earth. . . . All had wandered away from God : all had become abominable in their iniquities." But then came this new awakening : " God called men while they were still in their worst sins, and offered them new and hitherto unheard of methods of returning to Himself. New and unheard of, I say ; for who ever saw, who ever heard, in all the generations past, that kings, princes, mighty men of this world, puffed up with honours and riches, men and women of noble birth, should bind bridles upon their proud [and swollen] necks and submit them to waggons which, after the fashion of brute beasts, they dragged with their loads of wine, corn, oil, lime, stones, beams, and other things necessary to sustain life or to build churches, up even unto Christ's abode ? Moreover, while they draw the waggons, we may see this miracle that, although sometimes a thousand men and women, or even more, are bound in the traces (so vast indeed is the mass, so great is the engine, and so heavy the load laid upon it), yet they go forward in such silence that no voice, no murmur, is heard ; and, unless we saw it with our eyes, no man would dream that so great a multitude is there. When, again, they pause

[1] Compare Salimbene's description of " The Great Alleluia " in Northern Italy (A.D. 1233). This and similar revivals are described in chapter III of *From St. Francis to Dante*.

on the way, then no other voice is heard than confession of guilt, with supplications and pure prayers to God that He may vouchsafe pardon for their sins ; and, while the priests there preach peace, hatred is soothed, discord is driven away, debts are forgiven, and unity is restored betwixt man and man." . . . . As for the children, " you might see them, with their own little kings and leaders, bound to their laden waggons, and not dragging with bowed backs like their elders, but walking erect as though they bore no burden, and (more wonderful still) surpassing them in nimbleness and speed. Thus went they in a fashion far more glorious, holy, and religious, than any words of ours could express.

" When they were come to the church, then the waggons were arrayed around it like a spiritual camp ; and, all that night following, this army of the Lord kept watch with psalms and hymns. Then waxen tapers and lights were kindled in each waggon ; then the sick and infirm were set apart ; then the relics of the saints were brought to their relief ; then mystical processions were made by priests and clergy, and followed with all devotion by the people, who earnestly implored the Lord's mercy and that of His Blessed Mother, for their restoration to health. If, however, the healing were but a little delayed, nor followed forthwith after their vows, then all might have been seen putting off their clothes—men and women alike, naked from the loins upward, casting away all bashfulness and lying upon the earth. Moreover, their example was followed even more devoutly by the children and infants who, grovelling on the ground, not so much crept from the church porch upon their hands and knees, but rather dragged themselves flat upon their bodies, first to the high altar and then to all the others, calling upon the Mother of Mercy in the new fashion of prayer, and there extorting from her surely and forthwith the pious desires of their petitions. . . . Who indeed would not be moved, nay rather, whose stony heart would not be softened as he watched that pious humility of the innocent children dragging their naked ribs along the bare ground ? Who would not be pricked to tears by those lamentable voices crying aloud to Heaven ? Who, I ask, would not be bent by those tender hands and arms stretched out to be beaten with rods ? For it did not suffice them (though that surely were admirable at so tender an age !) to cry so long with the voice of weeping ; it did not suffice that so many tears should be shed ; but, of their own accord, they must needs add bodily pain also, to obtain the healing of these sick folk. The priests stood over them, shedding tears while they beat with their scourges upon the tender limbs thus exposed, while the children besought them not to spare their strokes, nor withhold their hand in too great mercy. All voices echoed the same cry, ' Smite, scourge, lash, and spare not.' . . . After each miracle a solemn procession is held to the high altar ; the bells are rung ; praise and thanks are rendered to the Mother of Mercy. This is the manner of their vigils ; these are their divine night-watches ; such is the order of the Lord's camp ; these are the forms of new religion ; these are the rites, the heaven-taught rites, in their secret watches. For here nothing carnal is seen ; nothing earthly of any kind ; all is divine, all is done as in Heaven ; heavenly altogether are such vigils, wherein nothing is heard but hymns, and lauds, and thanks."

It is a remarkable story ; and, in spite of the author's rhetorical style, we need not discount it more than we ordinarily discount the heightened colours of a tract written for edification. But we must look closely into Haymo's actual words, and pay special attention to certain points neglected by every author I have seen who refers to this treatise. In the first place, all this was part of a general and sudden religious revival in those particular districts—a spasmodic revival, suddenly waking people from their religious indifference. Secondly, Haymo knows no past precedent for this religious fervour in connexion with architecture. And, thirdly, in a later

part of his letter, he plainly implies that it was as sudden
in its passing-away as in its rise. He says in so many
words, concerning the dragging of chariots to the
Cathedral of Chartres : " He who hath not seen these
things will never see their like again." Yet in 1145 we
are only at the beginning of the great era of cathedral-
building ; this same popular effort which Haymo describes
at Chartres would have been welcome all through France,
not only during all Haymo's lifetime but far beyond.
We have, therefore, his explicit authority for treating
as exceptional and isolated phenomena the few scattered
notices which can be adduced from other sources as even
roughly parallel to this incident of 1145.

Here and there, as we have already seen in dealing with
Montalembert's evidence, a monk or a group of monks
are commended for their special enthusiasm in actually
helping the builders with their own hands. The author of
the metrical Life of St. Hugh of Lincoln tells us how, in
about 1190, " with wondrous art he built the fabric of
the cathedral, whereunto he supplied not only his own
wealth and the labours of his servants, but even the
sweat of his own brow ; for he oftentimes bore the hod-
load of hewn stone or of binding lime." Earlier than
this, in 969, the monastic chronicler of Ramsey lauds the
enthusiasm even of the hirelings : " These workmen
continued their labours as much from fervour of devotion
as from love of gain ; some bore stones, others made
mortar, and others again hoisted both on high by means
of a mechanical wheel, so that, the Lord giving increase,
the walls rose from day to day."[1] Again, not infrequently
the monks or canons contributed of their own money to
the building. At the Cathedral of Autun, in 1294, the
chapter taxed itself at 160 livres for the year ; and
93 livres of this were actually paid ; then again at 43 livres,
apparently all paid up ; the total receipts from all sources
amounted to 400 livres. At Troyes Cathedral, in 1380,
the only contribution of the kind was an entrance-fee

---

[1] *Hist. Rames.*, R.S., 1866, p. 41.

for each newly-elected canon of 13 livres odd.[1] At St. Albans, under Abbot John I (1195–1214), the monks gave up their wine for fifteen years in order to further the building of a new refectory and dormitory.[2] But the emphasis laid on instances of this kind is, to some real extent, a testimonial to their rarity. At Westminster, in about 1452, the new Abbot Millyng's " enthusiasm for the building was, as might be expected, reflected in sacrifices made by the monks themselves. They agreed each to contribute one mark a year towards the work, and to forgo entirely their annual visit to Battersea, for which the sum set aside was five pounds." This was for the building of the nave, to which Archbishop Langham, a former abbot, had contributed very liberally, and which was liberally helped also by Millyng's next successor but one, who from his own personal income, gave more than the equivalent of £6,000 modern.[3] " There are few things in the whole history of the monastery," writes Canon Westlake, " which make more pleasant reading " But when we remember that the abbot had a baronial income and lived in baronial state, and that the monks, vowed by their rule to poverty, were exceptionally well fed and clothed, and enjoyed their own private incomes, in defiance both of the Rule and of papal statutes, then the sacrifice is reduced to more ordinary proportions. Though these monks ceased, for some years, to indulge in a joy-ride and feast which cost the abbey about £2 per person in modern values, yet the Westminster customal, with numerous other documentary indications, show that their standard of comfort, even after this sacrifice and their money-contribution, would still remain that of a well-to-do merchant. Moreover, all that abbots and ex-abbots and monastery together contributed to this building, as a whole, was small indeed compared with the offerings of the royal family. Not long before this

---

[1] J. Quicherat, *Mélanges*, vol. ii, pp. 185 ff, 194 ff.
[2] *Gest. Abb.*, R.S., vol. i, p. 220.
[3] H. F. Westlake, *Westminster Abbey*, 1923, p. 192.

self-denial on the monks' part, Richard II had settled upon the fabric fund the whole revenues of one confiscated alien priory (Folkestone) and great part of another (Clare).[1] The Westminster walls were thus raised by money originally given by far-distant benefactors for widely different objects. And, though other sacrifices of this Westminster kind have sometimes been quoted, yet, when all are collected, they seldom or never give evidence for anything even remotely approaching the enthusiasm described by Haymo.

[1] Westlake, *l.c.*, p. 187.

CHAPTER XVII

ARCHITECTURAL FINANCE

LET us begin here with a perfectly typical instance for which a mass of detailed evidence survives, the great collegiate church of St. Victor at Xanten, on the Lower Rhine. At this city St. Victor was said to have been martyred in 286, with other comrades of the Theban Legion who refused to burn incense to the imperial gods ; and, according to a legend which meets us first in 1224, the church dedicated to him was founded by the Empress Helena. In Germanic legend the town is even more famous : " There grew up in the Netherlands a noble King's son, his father's name was Siegmund and his mother Siegelind, in a wealthy city, far and wide renowned, there on the Lower Rhine. Xanten was its name ; Siegfried was the name of that doughty warrior."[1] In the later Middle Ages it was one of the most prosperous towns on that great highway of commerce. The Provost of the Victorkirche was one of the outstanding ecclesiastical dignitaries of the province ; and the great church itself still survives as a monument of art. What is more important for our purpose, its records are extraordinarily abundant for the last four centuries of our period, and they have been worked through with exceptional diligence by Father S. Beissel, S.J. I cannot do better, therefore, than summarize here the sixty pages

[1] *Nibelungenlied*, Ab. II.

in which he deals with the finance of the fabric fund.[1]

How, he asks, did the Provost and Chapter raise that sum (equivalent to 3 million marks in the year 1889, or £150,000 sterling) which they spent on their great church between 1175 and 1560 ? And he enumerates the following sources.

(1) One of the prebends, on the foundation, had been assigned to the master-mason ; he received a canon's pay.[2] In 1374, the Chapter changed this ; the prebend was assigned to the building fund, and a separate agreement for wages was to be made whenever a master-mason was hired. This prebend defrayed about a quarter of the yearly expenses.

(2) The fabric fund had possessions of its own, from different benefactors ; in 1509 it possessed twenty-two houses, mostly in Xanten, and twenty-seven in 1547.

(3) If vicars or altar-priests chose to be non-resident, the Chapter applied to the fabric fund such sums as were offered at the absentee's altar. But there is no evidence that it took any of his regular income ; and Beissel notes that even the rule of partial confiscation seems to have fallen into abeyance.

(4) Fees for burial within the church ; or for ringing the great bell in honour of a funeral.

(5) The offerings at certain alms-boxes within the church.

(6) Frequent gifts from the Duke or Duchess of Cleves, when they came to Xanten.

(7) Contributions from the so-called Skittle-Gild (*Kegelgilt*), a social-religious brotherhood of extraordinary interest, though a full description here would take us too

---

[1] *Die Bauführung des Mittelalters*, Freiburg i/B., 1889. For this valuable book see farther in Appendix II. The present subject fills pp. 9–70 of part ii.

[2] And also, argues Beissel, a canon's full constitutional privileges ; but this seems very improbable, if only because the cup-bearer had also a full prebend, and the three cooks shared two between them, and the three bell-ringers shared another (I., 97).

far from our subject. Its activities ranged from policing the town (in virtue of a legendary grant from Constantine and his Empress Helena) to skittle-play and periodical feasts. " The canons took part in this game, to which they were very partial. The old Chapter statutes had indeed prescribed ' No member of the Chapter shall haunt taverns or play at dice or skittles ' ; but on the margin of this manuscript a fifteenth-century hand has written : ' That was no wise man who inserted this sentence against skittles ; for this is a decent bodily exercise, and one which holy and pious men use for their recreation.' " The entrance-fees for this gild went to the fabric.

(9) It became customary, at last, for all well-to-do folk to leave something to the fund at their death. Men often left their armour ; this was hung for view in the choir until a purchaser turned up, and a man was occasionally paid for scouring it from rust.

(10) It was common for sick folk to vow, for their recovery, their own weight in wheat to the fabric. The Duchess of Cleve, on one occasion, had herself weighed by the side of the common sufferers.

(11) Fines from evil-doers ; especially the frequent statutory fines imposed upon the clergy on duty when they came late for the services.

(12) " Conscience money," which is best described in Beissel's own words. " Archbishop Wilhelm v. Gennep [of Cologne] had indeed prescribed, in his diocesan statutes of 1354 and 1356, that all unjustly-gained possessions which were not to be restored to their rightful owners should be applied to no other purpose than the fabric-fund of Cologne Cathedral. But these prescriptions do not seem to have been legally binding in Xanten. For, on the one hand, the Chapter statutes commanded the master of the building-fund frequently to remind curates and chaplains who heard confessions in the church that. they must warn all penitents to apply such [ill-gotten] goods and their alms to the fabric of Xanten.

And, on the other, the accounts contain many items which show that these prescriptions were not without effect."[1]

(13) When there was a special call, the richer citizens met it promptly : e.g. in the crisis of 1463 we find " a considerable list of richer folk who gave from $7\frac{1}{2}d.$ to 15s. The town clerk is set down for 4s. 6d. . . . A poor woman gave him 13d., that the widow's mite might be represented also." But, in face of the fact that, in 1473, the best masons below the master received 3s. 9d. a day for their summer-wage, Beissel would seem a little over-enthusiastic over these gifts of 15s. from the richer folk.[2]

(14) For special emergencies, a general collection throughout the city. For instance, " In 1439, when one of the new bells cracked, the clerk of the works, Johann v. Goch, had it taken down and laid in the church. Then he ordered the carpenter to make a great chest by the *pulpitum* ; and, when it was finished, he called upon every body to fill it with kettles and pans that might be used for casting the bell again."

---

[1] Compare the following anecdote from Cæsarius of Heisterbach, who wrote about 1230 (*Dial. Mirac.*, dist. ii, c. 33). " There was at Paris a certain most wealthy usurer, Theobald by name. This man, having very many possessions and infinite moneys collected from usury, was smitten with godly compunction and came to ask counsel of Master Maurice [de Sully], bishop of that city [from 1160 to 1196]. He, being most fervent for the building of the Church of the Mother of God [i.e. Notre-Dame as we see it now], advised him to give his money to the fabric of that work. The usurer, having some suspicion of such counsel, went to Master Petrus Cantor [Precentor of Notre-Dame], and told him of the bishop's words. Petrus answered, ' This time he hath not given thee good counsel ; but go and let a crier call throughout the city that thou art ready to make restitution to all men from whom thou hast taken anything beyond thy bare capital.' He did thus ; and then returned to the Master saying : ' My conscience is witness that I have made all restitution to all who came unto me ; and I have yet many goods left.' Then said Petrus : ' Now thou canst give alms with a good conscience.' "

[2] It must be borne in mind that the different moneys in use at Xanten were far inferior in value to the English sterling coinage of the time, in spite of the similarity of names. So also with the contemporary French coinage.

(15) When these more ordinary sources were insufficient, they sold works of art from their treasury to be melted down. Thus, in 1422, they got leave from the Archbishop to sell in favour of the fabric fund " a little chest which is unnecessary for divine service, and which is only an ornament to our church. It is covered outside with gold and chased [or *embossed*], and some jewels are set therein." And they wrote to their agent in Cologne : " It is necessary to get this done quickly, before anyone else make any complaint, and thus (which God forbid !) may perhaps set a hindrance and a bar to our permission, as indeed is to be feared." It was broken up and partly sold in fragments to different goldsmiths, partly given in payment to separate creditors.

(16) They invested gifts and legacies in " rents " ; in other words, invested the money at interest, by a process which had been forbidden as usurious by earlier Church Law, but for which the more reasonable commercial ethics of St. Thomas Aquinas and his successors had by this time procured official allowance.

(17) They sometimes sent their officials to beg through the city, or even abroad as far as into Friesland.

(18) In their utmost extremity the Chapter intervened with its own possessions or income. In 1398 it gave 375 Mk. to the fabric fund ; and it often gave over to the clerk of the works a greater or less portion of the dues which it could claim from its serfs or subjects.

(*a*) Thus, the fund sometimes benefited by the bargains by which the Chapter sold to their serfs not indeed complete freedom, which was rare on the part of ecclesiastical landlords, but freedom from some of the most galling servile disabilities.

(*b*) This, however, still left the peasant subject to the " heriot," by which, when a man or woman died, the best beast, or other best possession, was taken as a fine by the landlord before he admitted the next heir to the holding. This, one of the most invidious of all feudal dues, brought in to the Xanten Chapter, in the single year 1468, 1,082½ *solidi*, equivalent to the average yearly earnings of four masons. Among the items thus taken from the peasants were gowns, beds, cows and horses; and we find only one excused altogether " because he was poor," while from two others, because they were poor, the Chapter took only 7½ and 9 *solidi* respectively, i.e. the price of a gown. A horse " of little value " was priced as low as 12, but they averaged about 50 and even ran up to 72. Cows averaged about 25 or 30. Of these takings the Chapter at first gave a certain proportion to the fabric-fund, but in 1485 and 1486 the whole.

(19) Letters of indulgence. " We find in the archives of Xanten a whole series of bulls of indulgence, wherein the pope and the bishops, in virtue of their plenary spiritual powers, promised and guaranteed the remission of all penalties for sin to those who helped the building of the Victorkirche with money or labour " (p. 27). The average income from this source in the early sixteenth century was nearly 100 Mk., or three times the yearly income of a master-mason.

(20) But, at frequent intervals, a special celebration was held, provoking special indulgences and contributions. This was called the *Victortracht*; relics were carried round, special services and solemn processions were held, the Duke and his family were invited, famous preachers were invited and entertained, and " two preacher-friars of Kalkar, Johann v. Bentheim and his companion, undertook to make the indulgences known in Holland and Friesland, for which the Chapter granted them 20 Mk. for their travelling expenses " (p. 69). This was a profitable outlay; they brought back 382 Mk. to the fabric. This was in 1487, the most elaborate Victortracht of all. The whole expenses this year amounted to 404 Mk., much of which went in wine to great folk and their servants; receipts came to 1,855 Mk., leaving a clear gain of 1,451 Mk.

In 1514 another offertory box was set up in the

Victorkirche, for those who wished to earn indulgences by contributing to the building of St. Peter's at Rome. Here, as Beissel points out, is a painful reminder of the great religious revolution ; three years later, the enormous extension of these indulgences provoked Luther's open resistance.

Brutails, again, has admirably analysed the finance of the fabric fund at St.-Michel-de-Bordeaux.[1] The town council voted a little money ; there was a Lententide sermon in aid of the work; there were certain collectors

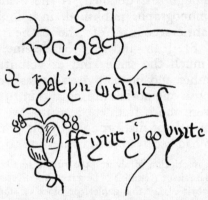

VOTIVE PILLAR-BASE AT BABRAHAM (CAMBS).

authorized to beg. The canons also distributed earthen-ware money-boxes which shopkeepers kept on their counters, from 15 to 20 dozen per annum. Here also, indulgences played a great part. At the cathedral, " the archbishops contributed to the repairs. The word ' liberalities ' has been wrongly applied here ; the fact is that this generosity was forced upon them by judges' authority ; the Chapter prosecuted them several times " (p. 24). One of the most abundant sources was that of testamentary legacies. A certain amount of work was given gratuitously by artisans. " Finally, there were the voluntary subscriptions of the parishioners. Some clubbed

[1] *Op. Cit.*, pp. 20 ff.

together to pay part of a workman's wages, just as nowadays, when a well-known church is being built, the faithful will offer a pillar, a stone, or so on.[1] Huguet Bauducheau, who has given his name to a street in Bordeaux, and several of his fellows received only part of their wages from the fabric-fund; the rest was paid by subscribers. One of these having ceased to pay his subscription, Bauducheau threatened to leave; the fabric-fund took over the subscriber's engagement in order to retain him " (p. 25).

Similar, though less detailed, is the evidence we get from three monographs published, in a limited edition, upon the fabric-accounts of the cathedral and the churches of St.-Jean and Ste.-Madeleine at Troyes.[2] They show much the same kind of voluntary subscriptions, in number and in relative value, as were raised for the different war-memorials in England in 1919. Legacies, of course, were more frequent; again, we get such an item as " a mantle of silk, brought by Sir Jehan Pougeoise [priest], who had received it in confession to be employed

[1] There is an inscription of about 1450 rudely scratched on the base of a pillar at Babraham (Cambs.) " Beverach and Kateryn Sant offyrit [offered] this gobyite," i.e. this goblet, or block of stone. The name Beverach occurs thrice in Bishop Brantyngham's issue-roll of 1370 (ed. Devon, 1835, pp. 28, 42, 311); this man was apparently a royal clerk. The heart seems to indicate that Beverach and Katherine were affianced or married. Compare the story in Cæsarius of Heisterbach (about 1230; dist. viii, c. 63). " There was a citizen of Cologne, rich and powerful, named Karl, father to the Lord Karl who was formerly Abbot of Villers. He, having heard that the Apostles would judge the world, said within himself: ' Sin is a heavy thing, and anchor-stones [probably the great basalt blocks which are quarried on the Rhine] are of great weight Therefore I will buy stones of that sort for the proposed building of the Apostelnkirche [at Cologne]; in order that, at the Day of Doom, when my good and my evil deeds are placed in the balance, these judges, the Apostles, may cast the stones into my scale that holds the good works, and they will forthwith weigh it down.' So he bought a shipload of stones, and had them carted and laid hard by the Apostelnkirche."

[2] (a) Comptes de l'œuvre de l'Église de Troyes; (b) C. de la fabrique de l'ég. St.-J.; (c) C. de la fabrique de l'ég. Ste.-M.; all published at Troyes by Bouquot in 1854 and 1855. The editor was Alex. Assier.

for the fabric-fund," which was sold at £2 10s. (a, p. 23). Indulgences, again, were a principal source ; Assier enumerates six bulls or episcopal letters to this purpose between 1415 and 1462, i.e. the period with which he is concerned for the cathedral. He writes (a, 57) : " The general ' pardons ' brought in to the Chapter consider-able sums, which the managers style ' recepte extra-ordinaire.' That of 1452 produced more than £1,000 [i.e. something like £6,000 in purchasing power at the present day]. Copies [of the bull] in Latin and in French were carried into the provinces ; friars preached in Lorraine, in Picardy, in the dioceses of Nevers and Reims and Soissons, and in Burgundy ; thousands of pilgrims visited the Cathedral of Troyes. Jean Belin, *miraclier*, furnished great *miracles à mirouer* [i.e. holy medals with a mirror], which were sent to pious sub-scribers. Day and night, confessors and preachers plied their holy office, the *miracliers* sold *miracles*, great and small, and gilded *enseignes* of St. Peter [to whom the cathedral was dedicated]. The preachers received gifts of Beaune wine ; the guardians and *miracliers* were fed with bread, wine and flesh at the expense of the fabric." At St.-Jean the church kept " fair garments of black damask and other stuff " which it hired out for funerals or weddings : " *Item*, received from Perrecin, that he might have the fair garments for the day of his wedding, 10 sols " (b, 22). And, contrary to the tradition among modern antiquaries that pew-rents date from the Refor-mation, these formed one of the most profitable sources at St.-Jean in 1508 (*ibid.*, 21).[1] So at St. Lawrence, Reading, " Seat rents appear to have been a source of church revenue from very early times. Anno 1441–2. ' Et de iiijd. de dono uxoris Johannis Tanner ptoj setell.' [' *Item*, of 4d. given by John Tanner's wife for a settle.'] A similar sum was paid by the wives of Robert Hover, John Strode, and Thomas Benham,

[1] For the antiquity of the pew-system, which in Italy dates at least from the twelfth century, see *Medieval Village*, pp. 252 ff.

but *6d.* was given by the wife of Nicholas Carter—for a *front* sitting no doubt. The seat rents in 1498 amounted to *6s. 6d.* The women only would appear to have been accommodated. The seatholders at this time were the wives of Thomas Smyth, . . . Hudson, 'bocher,' John Carpynter, the mother of Agnes Quedamton, the wife of Will. Hasylwood, John Ffauxbye, Will. Watts, Will. Jonson, Bartylmew Capper, Robard Dyer, John Darling, Will. Doyntre, baker, Mathew and Nicholas Goldsmyth.

1515–5. 'Also hit is aggreyd that all women that shall take any seate in the seid church to pay for the same seate vj except in the mydle range and the north range be neth the font the which shall pay but iiij and that every woman to take her place every day as they cumyth to church excepte such as have ben mayors wyfes.'

1520–1. 'Setis. *Item* of my lord (the abbot) for his moder sete iiijd.'

A touching entry. Hugh Farringdon, in his promotion to the abbacy, though a man of humble extraction, did not overlook, or forget to provide for, the comfort of his poor aged mother."[1]

We have seen how great a part was played by hired preachers and by licensed collectors who carried the church's wonder-working relics far afield. Two concrete instances will throw light on this system, which many good churchfolk reprobated as perilous and unedifying. The learned and pious Guibert, Abbot of Nogent in the early twelfth century, tells us of a fact within his own experience. The "most famous church" of which he here speaks is doubtless the Cathedral of Laon, close by his abbey, which was burned down in 1112 and sent round its shrine for help. We have a contemporary book of miracles performed by the shrine on this tour ; and it is noteworthy that the large majority of these belong to the three classes of miracle which Guibert exposes as most unsafe to trust in. He is himself writing an elaborate treatise *On the Relics of Saints*, and exposing the abuses

[1] C. Kerry, *Hist. of St. Lawrence, Reading*, 1883, p. 77.

which often crept in.[1] He proceeds : " But why do I
accuse the multitude, without citing specific examples
to rebuke this error ? A most famous church sent its
servants thus wandering abroad [with its shrine], and
engaged a preacher to seek alms for repairing its loss.
This man, after a long and exaggerated discourse on his
relics, brought forth a little reliquary and said, in my
presence, ' Know ye that there is within this little vessel
some of that very bread which our Lord pressed with
His own teeth ; and, if ye believe not, here is this great
man '—this he said of me—' here is this great man to
whose renown in learning ye may bear witness, and who
will rise from his place, if need be, to corroborate my
words.' I confess that I blushed for shame to hear this ;
and, but for my reverence of those persons who seemed
to be his patrons, which compelled me to act after thei
wishes rather than his, I should have discovered the
forger. What shall I say ? Not even monks (not to speak
of the secular clergy) refrain from such filthy gains, but
they preach doctrines of heresy in matters of our faith,
even in mine own hearing. For, as Boethius says, I should
be rightly condemned as a madman if I should dispute
with madmen."

In this light we may read that vivid picture from
Matthew Paris of the building at St. Albans under one
of its greatest abbots—John de Cella (1195–1214).[2] He
employed a too-ambitious master-mason, who tempted
him into great schemes, and " added carvings that were
impertinent, trifling, and costly beyond measure." The
work stuck half-way ; winter frosts came on and split the
unprotected stones ; the building began to crumble
away, " so that the ruins of the images and flowers moved
beholders to laughter and scorn. So the artists [artifices]
departed in despair, nor were they paid their wages for

[1] Migne, P.L., vol. clvi. col. 621 : Herman's *Treatise on the Miracles*
is *ibid.*, col. 963.
[2] *Gest. Abb.*, R.S., vol. i., p. 219. We must allow a little for Matthew
Paris's rhetorical style.

their work." The abbot appointed another mason, and assigned certain revenues to the fabric ; "yet that unlucky work never grew visibly . . . whereat he grieved inconsolably. Therefore he added many gifts of gold and silver, if perchance he might give increase to the work ; and he sent preachers throughout all the domains of St. Alban, and through many other dioceses, sending relics with them, and a certain clerk named Amphibalus, whom God, through the merits of St. Alban and St. Amphibalus, had raised from the grave after he had been four days dead, in order that he might supply ocular evidence for faith in the miracles of those saints ; by this means he heaped up no small sum of money. Yet that ill-fated work sucked up all this as the sea sucks up the rivers ; nor did the fabric yet grow happily." Even when the master-mason changed again, the church grew scarce two feet in height during thirty years. These relic-tours, therefore, were strongly deprecated by some of the more earnest church folk ; we have seen in Chapter XVI how Petrus Cantor complained that the great monastic buildings were frequently raised from the proceeds of usury or " the deceiful lies of hireling preachers."

This was a natural effect of medieval relic-worship. We may feel that Achille Luchaire, great scholar as he was, exaggerated in his dictum that " the real religion of the Middle Ages was relic-worship." Yet there can be no doubt that the cult of relics, in those days, played a far greater part than even in the least educated districts of Roman Catholic countries of to-day. We have already seen how that exceptionally popular relic, the corpse of Edward II, paid for all the new work at Gloucester and created a new style in architecture. Similar instances may be found down to the very end of our period. Two entries in Landucci's diary may here be placed side by side :—

" 12th June [1482]. At this time there was much talk of the worship of an image of Our Lady at Bibbona, or rather in a tabernacle about a bowshot from Bibbona. It is, namely, a Virgin seated and holding the dead Christ in her arms, after He has been taken down from the Cross ; which is called by some a Pietà. This worship began on April 5, when it was transfigured : that is, it changed from blue to red, and from red to black and divers colours. And this is said to have happened many times between then and now, and a number of sick persons have been cured, and a number of miracles been performed and quarrels reconciled ; so that all the world is running there. Nothing else is talked of at this moment ; I have spoken to many who tell me that they themselves have seen it transfigured, so that one must perforce believe it." The result was, that a church was built at Bibbona in honour of this image.

Then Landucci notes on June 19, 1484 : " In this July a worship of the Virgin Mary at Prato began ; people rushing there from all the country round. It worked miracles like that of Bibbona, so that building was done and great expense incurred." The further story of this building may be read in the editor's note.

Still more significant are the records of the indulgence-system. This is always in the foreground, even when we are dealing with cathedral cities of the first rank, populous and wealthy and marching in the forefront of the civilization of their age. The system had grown gradually ; but it had received a sudden and enormous impulse from the Crusades ; before the middle of the thirteenth century its obvious financial advantages had enabled it to strike root deeply and widely in every department of Church life. The greatest preacher of that century, Berthold of Regensburg, might complain publicly that thousands went to hell in the belief that they had bought remission of their sins " for a penny or a halfpenny " [1] ; but such objections had no appreciable effect ; rather the increase went on at an accelerated

[1] *Predigten*, ed. Pfeiffer, vol. i., p. 394 ; cf. 543 and *passim* ; or my *Medieval Studies*, 2nd ed., 1915, p. 24.

pace. At Sens, in 1295–6, the indulgences brought in more than one-third of the total receipts to the cathedral fabric fund.[1] At Evreux, they had begun at least as early as 1203, though in a rudimentary form. Innocent III, writing on behalf of the cathedral building fund " to all faithful Christians to whom these letters may come," continues : " We beseech you all, we warn and exhort you in the Lord, and enjoin upon you for the remission of your sins, to grant your alms, from such goods as God hath given you, for this rebuilding, in order that thereby, and by your other good deeds, ye may be able to attain to everlasting bliss." [2]   At St. Albans, about 1400, a monk drew up a list of indulgences obtainable at a single altar of the abbey church. He is apparently limiting himself to those granted in his own lifetime, yet these amount to nine.[3]   And he complacently describes a similar source of income, those " letters of fraternity " which Langland couples in his poem with papal indulgences.[4]   " Moreover, all benefactors who, from the goods God hath given them, pay anything for themselves or for those who are dear to them, living or dead, to the fabric of our Church, or of any of the abbey buildings or for the sustenance of the monks . . . become participants with us in the Masses which are daily celebrated by a hundred monks or more,[5] in their night-services and fasts and alms-giving and vigils, processions, scourgings, prayers both public and private, and all other [spiritual] benefits earned in this abbey or in the cells thereunto appertaining."   This system, reposing upon much the same

[1] M. Quantin, *Mémoires lus à la Sorbonne* (1868), pp. 209, 222.
[2] Abbé F. Blanquart, *Documents et bulles d'indulgences*, etc., Rouen, 1893.
[3] *Gesta Abbatum*, R.S., vol. iii, p. 544.
[4] See Chaucer, *Summoner's Tale*, and *Piers Plowman*, B. III, 47 ff.
[5] This number is greatly exaggerated for this date. King Offa, it is true, was said to have founded the abbey for 100 monks.   In about 1200 the *Gesta Abbatum* leave us to infer that, counting the dependent cells, there were about 100 in all.   But in 1380 we have the exact number, 56 (Dugdale-Caley, vol. ii, p. 209) ;   and at the Dissolution there seem to have been only 39.

theological presuppositions as that of indulgences, contributed powerfully to the commercialization of church-
building. It is not only that a Lollard like the author of
Piers Plowman's Creed draws some of his arguments from
the magnificence of the church and domestic buildings
of a Dominican friary, nominally vowed to poverty.
The very different author of *Piers Plowman's Vision*
confesses himself a grateful and obedient nurseling of
Holy Church. He had, again, a keen sense of beauty ;
some of his word-pictures are among the best that have
come down to us from the Middle Ages. Yet he is as
scornful as any Lollard in face of the false spiritual pre-
tences by which much of the money was raised for
building and adorning the churches which were being built
or rebuilt so busily in that age. His Lady Meed—the per-
sonification of ill-gotten gain, the Almighty Dollar of the
Middle Ages—makes neither profession of serious religion
nor promise of amendment, yet she has no difficulty in
making her peace with those who boldly claim to speak for
the Church.[1] She has only to confess herself to a friar and
give him a noble, or, in modern terms, a ten-pound note :—

" Then he absolved her soon ; and presently he said,
' We have a window a-working, will sitten us full high   [cost.
Wouldest thou glaze that gable, and grave therein thy name,
Secure should thy soul be heaven to have.'
' Wist I that,' quoth that woman, ' I would not spare
For to be your friend, friar, and fail you never . . . .
And I shall cover your kirk, your cloister do maken   [cause to be made
Walls do whiten, and windows glazen,
Do paint and portray, and pay for the making,
That every segge shall sayen I am sister of your house.'   [person.
But God to all good folk such graving defendeth,   [forbids
To writen in windows of their well-deeds,
Lest pride be painted there, and pomp of the world ;
For Christ knoweth thy conscience, and thy kind will   [natural
And thy cost and thy coveteise, and who the chattels owed.
Therefore I learn you, lords, leave now such works,
To writen in windows of your well-deeds,
Or to cry after God's men when ye deal doles,
Lest ye have your hire here, and your heaven also."

[1] B. III, 47.

Later, again, Langland returns to this subject, and shows us very clearly how thoughtful and earnest men regarded it in Chaucer's day. He obediently accepts the current theory of indulgences, little as he can reconcile it with other religious principles; but he is still more definitely convinced of an immutable moral law in the background (B. VII, 173).

" Now hath the pope power, pardon to grant the people,
Withouten any penance to pass into heaven ;
That is our belief, as lettered men us teachen
    Quodcwmque ligaveris super terram,
    erit ligatum et in celis, etc.[1]
And so I believe loyally (Lord forbid it else !)
That pardon and penance and prayers do save
Souls that have sinned seven sithes deadly.   [times
But to trust to these triennials, truly me thinketh, [three-year Masses
Is not so secure for the soul, certes, as is Do-Well.
Therefore I rede you, renkes, that rich be on this earth [counsel, fellows.
Upon trust of your treasure triennials to have
Be ye never the bolder to break the ten hests ;   [commandments
And namely ye masters, mayors and judges   [specially
That have the wealth of this world, and for wise men be holden,
To purchase you pardon and the pope's bulls.
At the dreadful Doom, when dead shall arise,
And come all before Christ, accounts to yield,
How thou leddest thy life here, and His laws keptest,
And how thou diddest day by day the doom will rehearse ;
A pocketful of pardon there, nor Provincials' letters,
Though ye be found in the fraternity of all the four Orders [of friars],
And have indulgences double-fold, but if Do-Well you help,
I set your patents and your pardons at one pie's heel ! "

Concerning which, scholars debate whether it is the last stale remnant of a pie-crust, or the heel of a magpie.

This brings us back to the indulgence-system proper. The matter can be studied most easily, for the later Middle Ages, in the Papal Registers. The British Government is gradually publishing a Calendar of these docu-

---

[1] Matt. xvi. 19. " Whatsoever thou shalt bind upon earth, it shall be bound also in heaven."

ments, whether Letters or Petitions, concerned with this country. From about 1300, when the entries begin to be fairly full, down to 1464, the date at present reached by the *Calendar of Papal Letters*, we may trace a steady increase in these indulgences for building. Let us take the last monastic and the last secular case recorded, both from 1462 (vol. xi, pp. 618, 636). On behalf of the monks of Christchurch in Hampshire Pius II grants an indulgence, " a relaxation in perpetuity of seven years and seven quarantines of enjoined penance," to all who, on certain two feast-days of the year visit the church and give alms for its repair. A like indulgence is given on behalf of the gild which has lately been founded in the parish church of Baldock for the maintenance of the fabric. Account-rolls sometimes tell us how much these papal grants cost ; the canons of Troyes, in 1382, paid 6 livres (about £25 in modern money) for one from Clement VII. The *York Fabric Rolls* give a whole collection of indulgences for the Minster fabric (pp. 158, 235 ff.) ; so do the muniments of every cathedral wherever they have survived. By the middle of the fifteenth century the system had reached vast proportions. Henry VI, in 1441, obtained the most generous indulgences for building his new collegiate church of Eton. A plenary indulgence, i.e. as much as could be obtained in past centuries by a crusade in Palestine, was now offered to all who, during the King's lifetime, should worship at Eton on the feast of the Assumption and contribute to the fabric. " Archbishop Chicheley wrote to the Bishop of Exeter ordering him to publish them in his diocese, and describing them as more ample than any hitherto issued by any pope. . . . It would appear that the payment made to the Roman Court ' for one Indulgence ' amounted to more than £158." [1] This kind of thing began to scandalize thoughtful churchmen still more. The greatest of Oxford Chancellors about this time was

[1] Issue Roll, Easter, 20th Hen. VI, quoted by H. Maxwell-Lyte, *Hist. of Eton Coll.*, 1911, p. 11. See Appendix 28.

Thomas Gascoigne, who wrote his *Liber Veritatum* about 1450. Here, he speaks very plainly about indulgences.[1] "I know that the officials of one cathedral church [viz., York], enjoin and command all parish priests in their province to bid their penitents, in Lententide, pay somewhat of their goods to the cathedral church; and the priest enjoins for a penance upon a poor man who has not fourpence, to pay forty pence to the Minster; and another priest has taken his own church and parish on farm from the Minster officials. I know one who pays five shillings a year to the Minster for his parish; and this very parish priest straitly enjoined upon every man in his parish that he should pay a certain sum that year to the cathedral church; so that certain poor folk paid to this priest forty pence [each] for the fabric, yet he who laid the injunction upon them had the parish to farm for five shillings." This, he tells us on another page, happened in about 1440; and he adds: "A doctor at the Council of Bâle wrote there a long discourse on papal indulgences, wherein he saith that he hath found no indulgences granted and sealed, after the fashion current in these days of ours, within the first thousand years of the Christian era; and that no saint ever expressed them in the form which is used nowadays. . . . Sinners nowadays [*moderni peccatores*] say 'I care not what and how many sins I commit before God's face; for I can get at once, with the greatest ease, plenary remission of any guilt and penalty by means of an absolution and indulgence granted to me by the pope, whose written grant I have bought for fourpence or sixpence or won as a stake at tennis.' For these indulgence-mongers scour the country, giving a letter [of pardon] sometimes for twopence, sometimes for a good draught of wine or beer, sometimes as a stake at tennis, sometimes for hire of a prostitute, sometimes for carnal love." Less than two generations after these words were written, the still busier trade in pardons for the fabric

[1] Ed. J. E. T. Rogers, pp. 1, 121, 151.

THE BUTTER TOWER AT ROUEN.

THE COBBLER ON THE CANON'S STALL.

of St. Peter's at Rome created the crisis which brought Luther forward.

Very similar was the system of selling relaxations of Lententide fast. At Mâcon, in Burgundy, in 1518, " the bishop granted permission to eat meat on Monday and Tuesday after *Dimanche Gras*, and milk and butter during Lent, to all who should contribute to the repair of the bridge. The same permission, again, was required by the inhabitants, on the same conditions, in 1547, 1548, 1549 and 1550. This shows that, even as late as this, the custom of abstaining from dairy-food during Lent, and from meat on Quinquagesima Monday and Tuesday, had not yet died out in the diocese of Mâcon." [1] A more striking example is the Tour de Beurre at Rouen, built between 1485 and 1597 from similar contributions. Ruskin, who was familiar with the tower and its story from his boyhood, wrote in later life : " It is ridiculous to attribute any great refinement of religious feeling, or height of religious aspiration, to those who furnished the funds for the erection of the loveliest tower in North France, by paying for permission to eat butter in Lent."[2]

Another source of income not infrequent, yet still stranger to modern ideas, was the system of fining unchaste clerics for the benefit of the fabric. I give many references on this subject in the notes to the last chapter of *From St. Francis to Dante*; another may be added here by way of illustration, from p. 314 of the calendar of the register of Bishop Stafford at Exeter (ed. Hingeston-Randolph, 1886). The bishop, visiting St. German's Priory in 1400, " found that John Pengelly, Nicholas Julyan, John Brystowe, and Bernard Page (*alias* Skelly), canons, had been guilty of scandalous and immoral conduct. He commanded each of them to be put to open penance. Pengelly was to sit on the floor in the middle of the Refectory, at meal time, and have nothing

---

[1] *Nouvelle Hist. de l'Abbaye de Tournus*, par un chanoine de la même Abbaye, Dijon, 1733, p. 246.

[2] *Works*, library ed., vol. xii, 1904, p. 45 note.

but bread and water, once in the day every Friday for seven weeks ; for a whole year he was to confine himself strictly to the choir and cloister, and not to walk about the road and speak to any women (whether of doubtful character or not), unless he had a trustworthy brother in his company ; he was not to undertake any manner of office within the said priory throughout the year ; and he was to forfeit out of his allowance for clothing one noble, to be expended on the fabrick of the Church : should he rebel, the Prior was to shut him up *in ergastulo ipsius Prioratus* [' in the prison of the said Priory '] for eight days, and allow him no flesh meat. Julyan was also condemned to sit on the floor of the Refectory ' duabus sextis feriis, inchoando die Veneris proximo post festam Sancti Michaelis Archangeli ' [' for two Fridays, beginning from the Friday next after Michaelmas '] and to have only bread and water once in the day : for a quarter of a year ' a festo Sancti Fidis ' [' from St. Faith's Day,' Oct. 6] he was to be confined to the cloister and choir ; and to forfeit 40*d*. out of his allowance for clothing, to be applied to the fabrick of the Church ; moreover, he was to sleep in the common dormitory. The same penance was assigned to Brystowe ; and Page was to abstain from fish and wine for two successive Fridays, and contribute 40*d*. to the fabrick fund. The Bishop wrote to the Prior (from Launceston Priory) September 18, requiring him to see to the execution of the sentence in each case, ' in virtute obediencie nobis prestite ' [' in virtue of the obedience rendered unto us ']."

We must therefore distinguish clearly, though not, of course, absolutely, between the short period or periods of enthusiasm and the long years of reaction or weariness. The records seem to show conclusively that such remarkable self-sacrifices as have been quoted on the part of monastic or cathedral chapters were, naturally enough, short-lived. Apart from these most remarkable buildings of all, which in France were mostly begun and ended within the single reign of Philip Augustus—apart, that is, from an architectural period which has no rival between the great Cluny revival and the still more epoch-making Renaissance—great medieval buildings often grew by fits and starts. Quicherat notes this at Troyes, and adds truly that we have here no isolated phenomenon. The step between Autun in 1294, when every canon was to pay something like 10 livres, and Troyes in 1380, when they simply imposed an entrance-fee on newcomers, is most significant.

Let us not fall, however, from the exaggerations of encomiasts into an equal exaggeration of unsympathetic criticism. The general medieval interest in building was, as I have noted already, quite as strong as the modern interest in machinery. Men's motives were mixed as they are now and always have been ; but the fact remains that the building or rebuilding of a church was generally, and perhaps always, a matter of strong local interest. We have an excellent example of this in the story of Bodmin. In vol. vii of the *Camden Miscellany* (1875) there is a most instructive account-book of the rebuilding of this parish church in 1469-71. " The whole sum expended," says the editor, " was £268 17s. 9½d. ; in addition to which, windows, trees and other materials, and labour were contributed." This cash, by itself, would be equivalent to about £5,000 at the present day. " Everyone seems to have given according to his means, and up to his means. Many who gave money gave labour also, many who could not give money laboured as best they might, and others gave what they could. We have gifts of lambs, of a cow, and of a goose ; and one woman in addition to her subscription sold her crokke [brass cauldron] for 20d. ; and all found its way into the common treasury. No age or sex seems to have kept aloof. We find a ' hold woman ' contributing 3s. 2½d. ; while the maidens in Fore Street and Bore Street gave subscriptions, in addition to the sums received from the Gilds of Virgins in the same streets. The Vicar gave his year's

salary, and the 'parish pepell' who lived in the town
contributed 19s. Much of the zeal shown may, we
think, be attributed to the influence exercised by the
Gilds." Of these religious gilds there were more than
forty in all. The accounts end up with a list of individual
contributors, 460 in all, which must have been nearly all
the adults in the little town, or perhaps quite all, since
it is evident that a quasi-compulsory collection was
voted ; a certain number are listed as defaulters (pp. 39-
41), and some are even distrained ; Joachym Hoper is
dead, and nothing can now be got out of him ; but from
John Harry, who owes two shillings, " a pot has been
taken, which is now with the mayor," and so on. We
must remember also that by this time a good many
church contributions, at first voluntary and individual,
had by long continuance become compulsory and universal ; this was one of the main complaints among layfolk in the early sixteenth century. We must remember
also that there was probably papal indulgence for all
contributing to this work—the Calendars of Papal Letters
unfortunately stop for the moment a few years short of
1469—and, certainly, all pious folk believed that the
contribution would mitigate their pains in purgatory.
But, after all legitimate discount, we have still a very
pleasant picture of a small community working together
at a common religious cause.

There is a pleasant sidelight, also, in the Xanten
accounts. We have seen how there was a chest into which
folk cast their old brass and pewter for the recasting of
the bell ; and the actual operation called forth a similar
effort. It was difficult to bring the furnace to the heat
necessary for so great a mass ; fresh bellows and fresh
smiths were hired from the neighbour city of Wesel, and,
in order to keep the blast constant for so many hours,
the local grammar-school boys were enlisted. " They
were paid in beer and cakes, while the ordinary work-
folk received bread and meat, or fish on fast-days."[1]

---

[1] Beissel, pt. i, p. 116.

But Beissel explodes the legend that the very asses contributed their labour to these holy causes, toiling up with their loads from stage to stage of the scaffolding. Jakob, the master-mason, did indeed raise all his heavy stones with the help of an *asinus*, but this was a sort of crane, named after the beast as the other is named after the bird ; it was probably what we see sometimes in old illuminations, a sort of gallows with horizontal beam and two wheels, not unlike the original velocipedes. In any case, its mechanical nature is proved by the fact that the clerk of the work accounts in 1356 " for the great pin for the wheel in the ass, 12*d.* ; item, for smaller nails for the ass, 14*d.*"[1]

It must be remembered, however, that religion was not the only force which kept men together. Patriotism, like religion, was in those days intenser in proportion as it was narrower. No unbaptized person, with infinitesimal exceptions which were practically neglected, could come to heaven ; all were enemies of Christ ; this gave a sort of artificial coherence to Christendom, though, even so, strict measures had to be taken against merchants and others who were ready, for the sake of gain, to supply the enemy even with materials of war. In the same way these smaller political units of the Middle Ages, in spite of their continual intestine quarrels, gained often a certain hysterical cohesion from their hatred and fear of the enemy outside. It is sometimes asserted that " nationalism " is a post-Reformation phenomenon ; it is not probable that any thoughtful person will believe this after reading Luca Landucci's diary, lately translated into English. This shows war as a chronic phenomenon in fifteenth century Italy, just as it had been for centuries before ; moreover, the loss of life and the bestialities were all the worse because it was not the larger area, " my country, right or wrong," but the smaller, " my province, right or wrong," and because a man could scarcely travel fifty miles from his own capital without coming upon

[1] Ibid., p. 102.

hostile soil. This it is which lends point to the words
with which Lambert of Ardres (about A.D. 1200) describes
the fortification of his native town in the Pas de Calais :
" The Count shut it in, and surrounded it himself with
a most mighty moat after the fashion of the moat at
St.-Omer, such as no hand had conceived hitherto in the
land of Guisnes, nor no eye had seen. Wherefore no
small multitude of workmen came together to make and
dig this moat aforesaid ; who, howsoever vexed by the
hardships of the season and pinched by the great famine
and afflicted by the labour and heat of the day, yet
chattered together and lightened their labour oftentimes with merry words whereby their hunger was
appeased. Moreover, many oftentimes came together to
see these great Earthworks ; for such poor folk as were
not hired labourers forgot their penury in the joy of
beholding this work ; while the rich, both knights and
burgesses and oftentimes priests or monks, came not
daily only, but again and again to refresh their bodies
and see so marvellous a sight. For who but a man
stupefied and deadened by age or cares, could have failed
to rejoice in the sight of that Master Simon the Dyker,
so learned in geometrical work, pacing with rod in hand,
and with all a master's dignity, and setting out hither
and thither, not so much with that actual rod as with
the spiritual rod of his mind, the work which in imagination he had already conceived ?—tearing down houses
and granges, hewing to the ground orchards and trees
covered with flowers and fruit, seeing to it with the utmost
zeal and care that the streets should be cleared, on work-
days even more than on holidays, for all convenience of
traffic, digging up kitchen gardens with their store of
potherbs or of flax, treading down and destroying the
crops to make straight the ways, even though some
groaned in the indignation of their hearts, and cursed
him under their breath ? There the peasant folk with
their mud-waggons and dung-carts, dragging loads of
pebbles to be laid upon the road, cheered each other to

the work with strokes and hearty blows on the shoulders. There, again, laboured the ditchers with their shovels, the hoe-men with their hoes, the pickers with their pick-axes, the beaters with their wooden mallets, the shavers with their shaving irons, and the stone-layers and wallers and rammers and paviours with their proper and necessary gear and tools, the load-men and hod-men with their hods, and the turfers with their oblong sheets of turf, cut and torn at the master's bidding from all the meadows around ; the catchpolls too, with their rods and knotted clubs, rousing the labourers and busily urging them to their work ; and ever in the forefront the masters of the work, weighing all that was done in the scales of their geometrical plan ; moreover, all these labourers were driven and constrained to this work through a continual time of travail and grief, of fear and pain." Writers have generally confined their attention too much to the great churches, and forgotten the villages and castles. Of all the writers on medieval art whom I happen to have read, Prof. Baldwin Brown is the only one who gives full value to the military side ; as indeed he is the writer who has gone most carefully to actual medieval sources, and taken most pains to verify his references.[1]

Finally, we must note that there is no evidence for the same healthy influence of public artistic opinion in the Middle Ages as in the Periclean Age. Not that there was no real influence, but the public was, so far as we can judge, far less sure of its own judgment and far less able to enforce this, than at the best periods of Greek art. *The Times Literary Supplement* for May 14, 1925 makes a significant comment on the attitude of Robert de Clari, one of the French barons who took and sacked Constantinople in 1204. " Characteristically, he is ignorant of the meaning and value of the classic art still preserved in the town, and is only interested in works of a supposedly miraculous nature. Santa Sophia, the chapel of the Emperors, the church of the Apostles, chiefly struck

[1] *Arts in Early England*, vol. i, p. 7.

his imagination ; but he describes in his naïve way many other things, including the equestrian statue of Heraclius, and the Hippodrome with its wealth of statues, which (Clari assures us) ' of old moved by magic, but nowadays never work.' To think of the last noble relics of classic Greek sculpture treated as examples of black magic and melted down to make bronze coins for these Frankish barbarians ! " In the matter of art, we cannot put the medieval knight or rich citizen side by side with the magistracy and aristocracy of Athens. Nor can we infer the same eager and critical attitude on the part of all the workmen themselves. Villard de Honnecourt shows us how masons discussed problems with each other ; but the gild system, while it kept the work up to a certain level, tended to discourage the highest originality. Apart from such limitations as we have seen Bishop Baldock imposing upon Tidemann of Germany, there is much significance in the German masonic statute of 1459, repeated later : " The mason shall in no wise blame his master's work, neither openly nor in secret—unless indeed the master work contrary to the ordinances of the Masons' Gild ; then may any mason speak against him."

CHAPTER XVIII

THE PURITAN REVOLT

I AM using the word *puritan* here in its purest and least invidious sense ; the sense in which it is applicable equally to St. Bernard and to Milton. I mean, the spirit which refuses to divorce art from morals ; which protests against being compelled to choose between the two ; and which, if so compelled, would attach even greater importance to morality than to art. This has been already anticipated to some extent in Chapter XVI ; in this present chapter, I shall deal more especially with the attitude of orthodox puritans towards Church images.

The equilibrium of thirteenth century civilization is often greatly exaggerated in our times ; especially the static and monumental character of the Church. That appearance of completeness and finality which Aquinas gave to Christian philosophy did not impose upon his contemporary Roger Bacon, who criticized the saint's work in very much the same terms in which Huxley might have criticized it. We have seen how doctors were burned or forced to recant at thirteenth century universities for saying very much the same things as pass from mouth to mouth in the sceptical circles of to-day. The fact that such recorded cases amount, perhaps, to less than a hundred at different times and places, is no proof that there were not far larger numbers who never fell into the hands of the authorities, or whose condemnation-records have not come down to us. Moreover, a still more significant fact, we have evidence for popular nonconformity growing *pari passu* with popular education. Expanding trade, wider experience of the world in general, swept away the narrower tutelage of the earlier Middle Ages. The original prohibition of usury broke down altogether ; entirely new definitions had to be framed in order to legitimize even ecclesiastical revenues ; a pope's definition conflicted with a saint's ; and, as trade and commerce still went on expanding, even the pope's and the saint's definition were commonly neglected. New growth was bursting old bonds everywhere ; many medieval ideals (as Bishop Lightfoot once put it) had already outgrown their strength before the thirteenth century was over. Art among others, and especially the imager's art, with accompanying image-worship, outgrew its strength.

The evidence I have already had occasion to quote may prepare the reader to learn, without surprise, that a good many of the best churchmen felt more and more serious misgivings in face of the popular imagery of their day. Things had been different in the past. Origen, the greatest of all the early apologists, had not only admitted the heathen accusation that Christians neither worshipped nor possessed images ; he actually gloried in the fact. Christians, he says, repudiate images for religious reasons : it was one of the Jews' great contributions to world-religion that they expelled from their state " all painters and makers of images . . . an art which attracts the attention of foolish men, and which drags down the eyes of the soul from God to earth." And, again, what reasonable man can refrain from smiling at these heathens, many of them even educated men, who " imagine that by gazing upon these material things they can ascend from the visible symbol to that which is spiritual and immaterial." [1] But this was about A.D. 240 ; and, some five centuries later, Pope Gregory II (or the official of

---

[1] *Contra Celsum*, Bk. IV, c. 31 ; vi. 14 ; vii. 44, 62-7 ; viii. 17-19. I deal with the matter more fully on p. 429 of *Five Centuries of Religion*, vol. ii.

the Roman Court who wrote in his name) argued complacently upon the assumption that the Apostles themselves had worshipped images.[1] For, by this time, the
historical facts were completely obscured by the current
practice ; nobody now cared for that ancient puritan
tradition, in a Church which welcomed imagery more
and more warmly in proportion as she found herself
confronted with the problem of converting, without
alienating, vast multitudes of heathens. Charles the
Great did indeed attempt to regulate this matter, just
as he strove to secure a pure text of the Vulgate Bible ;
nothing testifies better to this emperor's greatness than
his care for details both in Church and in State. " In
the image-quarrel, he took sides not indeed for the worship
of images, but for their retention [in the church]. ' Let
us not adore them,' he says expressly, ' but let us not
destroy them.' He even recommends their multiplica-
tion, not only to adorn the churches but also to commemorate great patriotic events. Yet he blames certain
iconographic eccentricities. Why should we represent
the earth and the moon in human form, or fashion double-
headed monsters, or fabulous creatures half-man, half-
beast ? ' That which is contrary to Scripture,' he writes
in a striking sentence, ' is contrary to nature.' Yet these
censures missed their mark, and the traditions against
which they were aimed persisted still for a long time in
iconography." [2] They persisted, as we shall see, until
the Reformation and the Counter-Reformation of Trent
agreed in condemning them.

The great medieval schoolmen were obliged to accept
past tradition as the basis of their philosophy ; not
necessarily the earliest Christian traditions, but such as
passed current in their own day because they came down

---

[1] The puritanism of primitive Christianity is brought out very strongly
by Remy de Gourmont, writing from a very different standpoint. He
claims it as one great asset of Roman Catholicism that it is " le christianisme paganisé " (La culture des idées, pp. 136, 149).

[2] André Michel, Histoire de l'art, tom. I, pt. ii, p. 939.

from their father's and their grandfather's day. There-fore the typical belief of the Middle Ages proper, even among the most learned churchmen, is that which we find in the *Summa Theologica* of St. Thomas Aquinas. He decides that " the same reverence should be paid to the image of Christ, as to Christ Himself. Since there-fore Christ ought to be worshipped with the adoration of *latria* [i.e. the adoration paid to God] it follows that His image should be worshipped with the adoration of *latria*." [1] And he backs this up with an historical asser-tion : " The Apostles, by the personal inspiration of the Holy Ghost, handed down for the observance of the Church certain things which they did not leave in writing . . . and, among these traditions, is the adora-tion of Christ's images. Wherefore St. Luke is said to have painted the image of Christ which is kept in Rome." St. Antonino, of Florence, in that *Summa Major* which was possibly even more read than St. Thomas in the later Middle Ages, repeats the same (pars. 3, tit. xii, cap. ix, § 1).

Yet, in face of what actually went on, misgivings some-times crept in. William of Auvergne, one of the greatest medieval bishops of Paris, writing about 1230, complains not only of the pagan idols still cherished by old women in his day, but also that, just as the ancient Greeks and Romans often thought their idols were gods, so " per-chance there are many simple folk also in our day who make no distinction in their prayers between the images of saints and the saints themselves ; nay, those prayers which they should make to the saints, they make to the images themselves." [2]   " There is another pagan super-stition," he continues, " the relics whereof subsist still among many old women even in Christendom.   For they say that all images acquire a certain virtue in the sixtieth

[1] *Sum. Theol.*, pt. iii q., xxvi, art. 3.   This orthodox philosophy rendered it difficult for later authors to explain why a piece of dead wood or stone must be worshipped with higher worship than the living Virgin Mary (Pelbart, *Pomerium*, lib. xii, pt. i, art. 1).

[2] This, as the author of *Dives and Pauper* points out (Com. I, c. 4), is sheer idolatry, whether it be done in ignorance or not.   See Appendix 29.

year from their [first] making, and keep it thenceforward
for so long as they endure ; to these images, therefore,
they have directed their censings and fumigations and
words and incantations as though these were true gods,
gods made with men's hands."[1]

Complaints increase as time goes on. Chaucer's friend,
Eustache Deschamps, wrote a balade on the theme " that
no graven images should be set in our churches, save only
the Crucifix and the Virgin, for fear of idolatry."[2]   In it
he writes : " For the work [of imagery] is a pleasing
shape ; the painting thereof, whence I complain, and the
beauty of the shining gold, make many inconstant folk
to believe that these are gods for certain ; and, in their
foolish thoughts, they serve these images which stand
around in the churches, wherein we place too many of
them. This is very ill done ; in brief words, we should
not have such images."

His contemporary, the friar who wrote *Dives and
Pauper*, blames the equivocal attitude of the official
Church towards the Cross, and says : " This blindeth
much people in their redynge [i.e. *interpretation*]. For
they meane [i.e. *think*] that all the prayers that Holy
Church maketh to the Cross, that she maketh them to
the tree that Christ died on, or else to the cross in the
church, as in that anthem, *O crux splendidior*. And so
for lewdness [i.e. *ignorance*] they be deceived, and worship
creatures as God Himself."[3]   Sacchetti, about the same

---

[1] *De Legibus* (*Opera*, ed. Regnault, Paris, 1516, vol. i, fol. 33, col. 3).

[2] *Œuvres* (Soc. d'anciens textes français), vol. viii, p. 201.

[3] Com. I, c. 4 (ed. Berthelet, 1534, f. 15.v°).   Cardinal Gasquet, on
p. 75 of his *Monastic Life in the Middle Ages*, quotes this author as *dis-
proving* the Protestant delusion that, " by allowing this customary reverence [to the Cross], the Church had given occasion for the growth of
serious superstition among the common people, amounting in reality to
practical idolatry."   In order to make out his case, he quotes the words
of *Dives and Pauper* which precede and succeed this frank admission on
the author's part, but *suppresses the whole of the passage which I here quote
in the text*, and gives no reference which would enable the reader to check
an omission which he marks by only three dots.   See Appendix 29.

time, was preaching against similar abuses. The Holy Crucifix of Lucca, though its hoary antiquity gave it surpassing virtue in the minds of such old women as William of Auvergne rebuked, and such semi-pagans as our William Rufus, and such sinners as Dante satirizes in the twenty-first canto of his *Inferno*, was estimated at its true value by this intelligent and plain-spoken Florentine novelist, Sacchetti. This fashion in images, he writes, this attribution of more virtue to one than to another, is sheer idolatry ; so far is it from edifying, that it makes reasonable men doubt of the faith ; the Perugians believe more in their Sant' Ercolano than they do in Christ ; the vicious system is encouraged by priests and monks to bring grist to their own mill.[1] This last accusation is borne out by Church councils of about the same time.

Roughly contemporary with Sacchetti, again, was the Bohemian Mathias von Janow, often called Mathias Parisiensis, because he had been professor of divinity at that university. To him (about 1370), the question of church images is already among the most serious. He writes :

" Alas ! nowadays certain associations [*collegia*], and the multitude of those who call themselves masters of the Church and wise men, have decreed in God's name in the Church [*decreta Dei in ecclesia posuerunt*] to the effect that images of wood or stone or silver or such like should be adored and worshipped by Christians, though Holy Scripture saith openly and expressly, ' Thou shalt not adore nor worship them ' ! a thing which can by no means be held or defended from the assertion of Thomas Aquinas or from other doctors ; *and Holy Church, although she has admitted images and statues to be honoured and reverenced, yet she has never taught or decreed that they should be adored or worshipped*, as may be seen in the Corpus [of Canon Law], in the Faculty of Law. . . .

---

[1] *Sermoni*, Florence, 1857, pp. 214 ff. ; Novella, 157 *ad fin* ; Novella, 169. I give this evidence and that of the Councils more fully in *From St. Francis to Dante*, 2nd ed., pp. 309 ff. and notes.

They have decreed also, and have commanded in their synods that men should preach to the people, *that folk may piously believe God's virtue, and the virtue of the saints, to reside in painted images of stone or wood,* and therefore that the miracles which are seen or reported to be wrought by them are wrought by God through and on account of these images ; and therefore whosoever believes this, or puts faith in such an image and takes refuge in it doeth no wrong ; nay, they say it is impossible that he should do wrong, nor are simple folk to be corrected and rebuked for fleeing to images in times of their need, or to relics of the saints or other such dead things that have neither merit nor virtue. Moreover, they have decreed that we should not preach against such abuse of statues or relics ; for they say that Christian folk do not err in such matters. Yet who doth not understand how pernicious these things are to rude and carnal Christian folk, if only he reflect how the common folk of to-day, not having the spirit of the Lord Jesus, can by no means be raised in mind to spiritual things, but, impelled only and chiefly by carnal judgment and fancies, they prize only bodily things, and marvel and fear in the presence of such things, pouring out their whole soul to these things."[1] In another place he points out how, in comparison with famous statues like the Holy Rood of Lucca, "men pay slight attention, or none, to the Body of Christ, present in the same place. The reason whereof is that the unlearned people, following their senses only, are strongly moved by such images and by their splendid and artificial appearance ; and that all such folk are prone to idolatry, seeing that they circumscribe their concepts or their imagination more easily, and limit it more gladly, in the creature than in the Deity, since the creature is nearer to their natural faculties. . . . Yet by this I intend not to deny that images may reasonably be made and

---

[1] F. Palacky, *Die Vorläufer des Husitenthums in Böhmen*, Prag, 1869, pp. 78–80. The sentences I have here italicized have been marked by Lord Acton in his copy.

placed in the church, since all Holy Church holdeth thus, and men commonly say that such images are the lay folk's Bible. Let the Church, therefore, be adorned with statues ; I oppose not this, nor gainsay in any wise, provided that we be on our guard against the devil's wiles here as in other things." And elsewhere the author speaks even more plainly for his orthodox intention : " I submit these words, all and several, and myself also, to the Holy Catholic Church, my most sweet mother, and bride of Jesus Christ."

THE TRINITY AND THE FOUR
EVANGELISTS
(FROM A BOOK OF HOURS).

St. Bernardino of Siena (d. 1444) was distressed by remnants of pagan superstitions among the worshippers at St. Peter's in Rome, and indignant that such open sinners as usurers should treat the images as other folk did and do still, " defiling the saints painted on the walls by touching their countenances with shameless hands and then rubbing over their own faces." [1] His older contemporary, Cardinal Pierre d'Ailly, one of the greatest figures at the Council of Constance, propounded to that Council, among other necessary articles of reform, " that so great a variety of images and pictures should not be multiplied in the churches." [2] A few years later, the still more distinguished Cardinal Nicolas of Cusa, as bishop of

[1] *Opera*, ed. de la Haye, vol. ii, pp. 53, 256.
[2] V. d. Hardt, *Mag. Œcum. Const. Concilium*, vol. i, p. 423.

Brixen, complained that the Tyrolese, his flock, " generally " worshipped the saints only for selfish and material reasons, " for the prosperity of their crops and their herds," and therefore witchcraft was particularly abundant in those mountain districts.[1] As Papal Legate in Holland, he publicly proclaimed that " to call upon this or that saint for this or that thing, is a relic of paganism." [2]

The idea that the average church building of A.D. 1500 was filled with imagery presenting an harmonious body of teaching, is quite anachronistic.[3] We have abundant indications, slight enough individually yet convincing in their totality, that, where there was not great neglect, there was often great confusion. Very significant is a Lincolnshire document of about 1480 printed by Trice Martin in *Archæologia* (vol. lx, p. 366). It is a petition to Chancery ; i.e. a protest against the strict law and an attempt to secure the King's protection in the name of equity. The first half runs : " All the parishioners of Grayingham, near Kirton in Lindsey, who are tenants of our Lord the King, beseech that, as a dispute has arisen between Robert Conyng, parson of one half of the church of the said town of Grayingham, and the said parishioners, touching an image which the said Robert has had set in a place within their said Church to the great nuisance of the said parishioners, so that they cannot well see the

---

[1] Van Steenberghe, *Nicolas de Cues*, p. 160.

[2] F. A. Scharpff, *Nicolaus v. Cusa*, Mainz, 1843, p. 181. On this point the reader may find a mass of interesting details in Dr. van Gennep's *Essai sue le culte populaire des saints franciscains en Savoie* (*Rev. d'hist. franciscaine*, Avril–Juin, 1927, pp. 113 ff.). He shows that in this district, which he knows intimately, the cult of saints is prevalently utilitarian ; those survive who have the reputation of curing some constant and frequent trouble among the country folk. Thus " St. Antony of Padua has succeeded in keeping his place, because he was the first intercessor who specialized in the recovery of lost articles. And, since mislaying is a durable and widespread defect, therefore St. Anthony of Padua retains really popular worship in parts of Savoy, whereas St. Francis of Assisi and St. Clare have fallen into oblivion, except, perhaps, among the educated middle-class and the lower local nobility."

[3] Unless, of course, it had been newly built or restored.

elevation [of the Host] nor divine service performed in the said Church. And because they would complain of it, he has caused to be denounced as excommunicated all the said parishioners who would gainsay him or hinder him in his will in this behalf. And because they have obtained an inhibition of the said denunciation from their Archdeacon, the said Robert has summoned the said parishioners to be before the Bishop of Lincoln within a short time to come, to bring them into court and vex them as much as he can of his malice."

We need not wonder that, while high ecclesiastics murmured their misgivings, common folk were saying the same things more and more insistently and with less and less ecclesiastical caution ; and here was one of the currents which led to the religious revolution of the sixteenth century. Then it was that the miracle-play and the image went through the furnace of affliction. In 1565, St. Charles Borromeo forbade the Passion Play altogether, and all other theatrical representations on Church Holy-days, throughout his province of Milan.[1] Pope Urban VIII, in 1628, forbade at last such representations of the Trinity as had scandalized Wyclif two hundred and fifty years earlier ; he prescribed, under penalty of anathema, that all figures should be burnt which portrayed the Three Persons " in the shape of a man with three mouths, three noses, and four eyes." Benedict XIV, in 1745, recalled and confirmed this condemnation.[2]

What, then, had caused this change in the orthodox attitude towards medieval symbolic art ? The story is admirably told by Mâle in his concluding chapter (vol. iii, pp. 525 ff.) ; yet we may be permitted to add a little to what he says, and to suggest certain points of view which he scarcely treats with full justice.[3]

[1] Dejob, p. 212.
[2] Didron, *Christ. Icon.*, vol. ii, p. 61.
[3] Very useful also is a much smaller volume by Dr. Charles Dejob. *De l'influence du Concile de Trente sur la litt. et les beaux-arts chez les peuples catholiques*, 1884.

Nearly all the heretics (he points out), like nearly all the orthodox reformers, had taken a puritan view of art. But the heretics had, of course, gone farther, and repudiated the whole system of ecclesiastical imagery. Thus the leaders of the Counter-Reformation, the fathers of the Council of Trent, had to deal with the acknowledged abuses of images, while they insisted on their use. In their twenty-fifth and last session, after formally anathematizing all who denied purgatory, they cursed with equal solemnity all opponents of images. After this the decree proceeds : " Yet, if any abuses have crept into these holy and salutary observances, this Holy Synod is vehemently desirous of abolishing such altogether, so that no images of false dogma may be set up, giving occasion of perilous error to simple folk. And if ever it chance that stories and narrations of Holy Scripture are sometimes expressed and figured, as this is expedient for the unlearned multitude, let the people be taught that the Deity is not figured on this account, as though It could be seen with the bodily eyes, or expressed in colours or shapes. . . . Moreover, let all wantonness be avoided, so that images be not painted or adorned with provocative beauty." This was in November 1563 ; and in 1570 appeared the book of Molanus, " *Concerning Pictures and Sacred Images*, treating of the Avoidance of Abuses with Regard to them, and of their Signification." A posthumous edition, with fresh matter, in 1593, was entitled " *Of the History of Holy Images*, for their true Use against Abuses, in four Books." The author, whose native name was Ver Meulen, was professor at Louvain, and of a learning which impressed the learned Baronius. Writing in the face of heretics, he is concerned to emphasize those apologetic words of the Council " if any," " if ever," and to insist that the worst abuses of which he speaks are rare (p. 228). Again, after describing several types of picture, he is careful to add his opinion that, though reprehensible, they are not actually such as to " give occasion of perilous error to simple folk " (75). Later on, it is true, he is less definitely on the defensive, and reminds his readers how the St. Christopher guarantee had lately been condemned at a provincial Council as " an abominable vanity and superstition " ; but we shall understand his attitude best if we look first at these earlier instances which he does indeed blame, but refuses to bring under the anathema of the Council, and denies to the parish priest the right of making any change except by authority of his bishop. And, farther to understand this question, we must bear in mind that Molanus was evidently not an artistic nature, and that he deals with the subject from the point of view of the ordinary theological professor of the Counter-Reformation.

"I think" (he writes, p. 70) " that there is not even one [image which gives occasion of error to simple folk] in our Churches, although they seem, or at least might seem, such. For in certain places, in the story of the Annunciation and the Lord's Incarnation, there is painted a little human body, among rays diffused by the Holy Ghost, descending to the most blessed Virgin's womb ; which picture might seem to offer an occasion not only of perilous but even of heretical error. For Valentinus has long been held a heretic by the Church, for teaching that Christ brought His body from heaven, and passed through Mary only as through a pipe ; wherefore St. Antonino [1] doth sharply reprove this picture, saying ' reprehensible, also, are painters who paint things contrary to the Faith ; when they represent the Trinity as one person with three heads, which is a monster in nature ; or, at the Annunciation, a little fully-formed child, Jesus to wit, sent into the Virgin's womb, as though His body were not taken from the substance of the Virgin ; or the child Jesus with a hornbook, whereas he learned not

[1] The great Dominican teacher, Archbishop of Florence, 1448-59, whose authority on moral questions was perhaps even more studied, in the later Middle Ages, than that of Aquinas. The quotation is from his *Summa*, pars. iii, tit. viii, c. 4, § 11.

from man.'[1] Again, at the Last Judgment, some portray the
Blessed Virgin and the Baptist in prayer, a representation
which would seem to savour of what St. Augustine hath condemned, to wit the dogma of the salvation of the damned
through prayers and intercession of the saints, and to
be in direct contradiction to Gratian [cause xiii, q. 2][2]. . . .
Again, some portray the Archangel Michael with scales,
weighing the soul in one and its virtues in another.
They represent the Devil standing at the soul's scale and
striving to press it down in so far as he can ; while, on
the other side, Michael with his sign of the Cross hinders
the Devil's attempt, and seems to add something more
to that scale from the merits of Christ's passion and cross.
But from such a representation some would easily infer
that those attain to eternal life whose good works outweigh the bad, while those in whom the bad outweigh
the good are left to the Devil.[3] . . . Moreover, some

---

[1] To this St. Antonino himself adds : " Nor are they praiseworthy when
they paint apocryphal things, as the midwives at the Virgin Birth, or the
Virgin Mary at her Assumption leaving her girdle to the Apostle Thomas by
reason of his doubting, and things of that sort. Also when in the stories of
saints or in churches they paint curiosities which avail not to excite devotion, but laughter and vanity, as apes, and dogs chasing hares, and so forth,
or vain ornaments of apparel, this seemeth superfluous and vain."

[2] Molanus seems here to have lost hold of medieval symbolism ; for
the praying St. John is generally the Evangelist and not the Baptist,
though by no means always, especially in Germany and the Netherlands.
Mâle, who notes Reims as an exception in France, holds that the German
examples teach another story ; not intercession but : " Here is He whom
I foretold." Yet on the main point he agrees with Molanus (II, 472).
" The theologians had affirmed that, at the Last Day, no prayer could
move the Judge ; but the humble crowd of the faithful did not believe
this. They continued to hope that, at that day, the Virgin and St. John
would still be powerful intercessors, and would save more than one soul
by their prayers."

[3] The annotator quotes here an example of such interpretation, from a
medieval Dominican legend. A usurer, in a vision, saw his soul thus
weighed by Michael ; the vices were " infinitely heavier " than the virtues ;
only he had been accustomed to say the rosary of the Virgin Mary every
day. Therefore she now intervened, cast a rosary into the lighter scale,
and the heavier at once kicked the beam. The usurer was converted by
this vision to amendment of life.

represent St. John the Evangelist as the spouse at the marriage-feast of Cana. Yet, as Catharinus saith, we must by no means believe that he was the spouse at that wedding whereunto Jesus was called ; for in that case our Lord would have dissolved the marriage ; yet He came, as holy expositors rightly teach us, to honour and approve it. If, on the other hand, He had dissolved it, He would rather have supplied the heretics with an argument for disapproval of marriage. To this we may add that Salome, mother to the sons of Zebedee, coming to Christ with her sons the Apostles James and John, is [sometimes] portrayed bringing her sons like little children to Christ. For from this picture it would seem that a man might well argue : ' Lo ! Christ chose children for Apostles, for these were the two against whom the ten were angry : wherefore then should it not be lawful to give Church benefices to children ? ' And, lastly, that Charles Martel, that great Duke of Brabant who was grandfather to the Emperor Charles the Great, is painted as receiving imposition of hands or absolution from St. Giles ; or, as another representation hath it, an angel announceth to Charles the remission of his sin, with a verse added :

Aegidii merito, Caroli peccata remitto,[1]

which seems to answer to that story of St. Giles wherein it is written that, at the revelation of an angel, and at the prayers of St. Giles, this King of France . . . was forgiven a great crime, which he had not dared to confess to any man, on condition that he should desist therefrom for the future. And that this was added at the end : Whosoever should call upon St. Giles, for whatever sin, if he ceased from the practice thereof, then he might believe without doubt that God had forgiven it him. But, seeing that this story is partly in contradiction with Holy Scripture and Church tradition, which demand sacramental absolution, it would seem also that the image which expresseth

---

[1] " By the merit of Giles, I remit Charles's sin."

this story should be relegated among those which give occasion of error to simple folk."

The extreme caution of the conclusions here drawn by Molanus (he will not say that these things *do* fall under the Council's anathemana, but they *seem* to fall) and the care with which he proclaims the subordination of his own judgments to those of popes or bishops, whenever popes or bishops might see fit to pronounce themselves, lend all the more significance to these examples which he quotes. Moreover, the reader will see that, in two at least of these cases, what he reprehends is not rare, as in his apologetic mood he had pleaded, but normal and almost universal. Mary and John praying at the Doom, with Michael weighing the souls, are among the most unchanging features of medieval symbolism. Yet all these he would willingly sweep away.

He refuses to go so far as Erasmus in reproof ; yet he realizes how many artistic conventions repose on popular imagination (90). And on one point he agrees with Erasmus, in his *Institution of Christian Matrimony*, though he knows that the book has been condemned by the Council of Trent. He entirely disapproves of unnecessary nudities, e.g. David and Bathsheba, or Salome dancing alluring dances before Herod. He transcribes Erasmus's blame of the farcical element introduced by artists ; " as, for instance, when they portray Mary and Martha receiving our Lord to a feast, the Lord speaking with Mary, and John as a youth talking secretly in a corner with Martha, while Peter drains a tankard. Or again, at the feast, Martha standing behind by John, with one arm over his shoulders, while with the other hand she seems to mock at Christ, unaware of all this. Or again, Peter already rubicund with wine, yet holding the goblet to his lips." These were probably the extravagances of Flemish painters.

More serious are his criticisms of the scenes from Christ's, or Mary's, life. He realizes that the former sometimes come from the apocryphal *Book of Christ's*

Infancy (83). He reprobates the figment, based upon this same book, that Mary was conceived by the kiss of Joachim and Anne at the Golden Gate (393). He approves of the attempts to follow definite and ancient tradition of portraiture, especially in these holiest pictures of all ; but here he has to wrestle with the discordance of early written authorities (164). Epiphanius had described Mary as " of a colour that recalled wheat, with yellow hair and keen eyes, of a yellowish hue and as it were oil-coloured in the pupils." A Greek of the eleventh century described her as " somewhat dark [*subfusca*], with tawny hair and tawny eyes " ; yet Pelbart, in the fifteenth, is certain that she was dark-haired.

It would be too long a task to follow Molanus farther through his iconographical difficulties ; but here again we must note how careful he is to give no handle to iconoclasm (84). " It seemeth to me (yet I subject mine opinion to the correction of others), that it is not expedient to remove or change pictures of this sort, if some folk's weakness would be troubled thereby, so long as no provincial synod decrees otherwise in that particular case. Let us tolerate and permit some things for the sake of the weak, even as our Mother Church tolerates and permits certain things. How many opinions does she tolerate in published books ? She tolerates *Vitaspatum*,[1] though Pope Gelasius and his council once reprobated the book.[2] She tolerates Jacobus de Voragine's *Golden Legend*, which some men call *The Leaden Legend* ; for, as Melchior Cano saith, ' This book was written by a

---

[1] A collection of stories of the early Fathers of the Desert, varying much in date and in authority, which the Middle Ages regarded as the foundation of monastic history. An English version of a Syriac redaction of this collection has been published by E. A. Wallis Budge, 1907.

[2] The reference here given is to the first volume of the *Corpus of Canon Law*, Gratian [pars. i], dist. xv. But I can there find no mention of this book in the long list of volumes reprobated ; on the contrary, the list of books recommended contains certain lives extracted from the kernel of this book. The other list, however, contains the name of Cassian, and Molanus may be thinking of this.

man of iron mouth and leaden heart, and certainly of small gravity or prudence in mind ' ; words which he hath borrowed from Ludovicus Vives. She tolerates much which hath been already published in divers histories, things uncertain, fabulous, apocryphal and lacking all verisimilitude, only taking care that they be not read in Church. . . . Therefore, that which the Church tolerates in books, let us also, with her, tolerate in pictures, which the Fathers have justly named the Scriptures of the Simple. Meanwhile let the simple be taught what they ought to learn, what not to learn, from images of this sort. Let painters and sculptors be taught to avoid at least the more notable and important errors in that which they set up. This, after all, is easy, since the more notable errors scarcely exist except in images which, when all things are considered, are rare."

CHAPTER XIX

REFORMATION OR RENAISSANCE ?

MUCH of the evidence given in Chapter XVIII is rehearsed more briefly in Mâle's concluding chapter, entitled : " How did Medieval Art End ? " Since my own answer to that question differs on some important points from his, it is the more necessary to present his point of view fairly.

" It seems," he writes, " that the rich iconography [of the Middle Ages] had never been more living and fertile than at the beginning of the sixteenth century. How is it then that, a few years later, it dissolved and soon disappeared without leaving any traces behind ? The first idea which occurs to us is, that the medieval tradition in France was killed by the art of the Italian Renaissance." At first sight, we say that the mark of medieval art was humility ; as for that of the Renaissance, " its hidden principle is pride ; henceforth man is self-sufficient and aspires to be a god." This art did indeed come into France with Francis I, and conquered rapidly : " but this new conception of art did nothing to modify the old iconographic dispositions." Mâle gives examples of a Nativity and an Assumption, and concludes : " Thus Italian Renaissance art, penetrating into France, did nothing to destroy the old French iconography ; it conformed itself thereunto. . . . If the tradition of the Middle Ages is dead, the slayer is not the Renaissance, but the Reformation. It is the Reformation which, by compelling the Catholic Church to watch every aspect of her own thought and to concentrate herself violently, put an end to that long tradition of legends and poetry and dreams."

How is this ? " One of the first consequences of the Reformation was to render Catholics suspicious of their old religious drama. They perceived for the first time that the authors of the miracle-plays had mingled the Gospel text with a thousand fables, a thousand platitudes, and a thousand coarsenesses. They had to admit that the Protestants were not altogether wrong in saying that these detestable poets ' changed the holy words of the Bible into a mere farce.' The happy age of innocence, in which everything is graceful, was now past and gone." The municipality of Amiens raised difficulties in 1541 ; the Parlement of Paris, in 1548, expressly forbade the gilds to represent " the mystery of the Passion of our Saviour, or other sacred mysteries." The miracle-play lingered on here and there, but the edict of 1548 had given it its death-blow. And " its disappearance had serious consequences for Christian art. We have shown how the mystery-plays had in a great measure created the iconography of the later Middle Ages. . . . When they disappeared, no traditions remained but those which lingered still for a while in the workshops. . . . Thus, by the end of the sixteenth century, our artists suddenly found themselves facing the subjects of Christian art without traditions [to guide them]. Their pride was doubtless flattered by this ; for Italy had taught them that a great artist owes no debt but to himself ; yet Christian art did not gain by this. In that dying tradition there was more poetry and tenderness and pain than any man, even a genius, could put into his work. That is how the Reformation, by killing the medieval theatre, struck an indirect blow at iconography." And, at this very moment, in 1563, came that decree of the Council of Trent which regulated Church images. " There was a fresh consequence of the Reformation. The Protestants had declared war against images, and they must not be permitted to have legitimate motives for mocking the

credulity of the Catholics or their want of moral deli-
cacy." The clergy were still the guides of the artists ;
" but one thing is evident, that this clergy felt none of
the scruples which the Reformation awoke in men's
minds." Canons and bishops saw no reason why pagan
legends, even Mars and Venus or Bacchus and Ceres,
should not figure in churches. Again, " nothing testifies
more clearly to their tolerance than those [carved] stalls
of the fifteenth and sixteenth centuries. There is no
room in them for things of heaven ; they represent daily
life "—the water-carrier, the tallow-chandler, etc. ; or
again, fairy-tales or satirical fabliaux. It is a mistake to
suppose that these things were done behind the backs of
the clergy ; in 1458, for instance, the canons of Rouen
were shown by Viart, in his workshop, specimens of the
little grotesques with which he adorned the still-existing
stalls of the cathedral, " and they went away thoroughly
satisfied."

Such was still the orthodox mind about 1530. " Everything beautiful deserves to be gratefully received. Beauty
is heaven-sent ; every fair work, be it pagan or Christian,
is a message from God. Had not the Pope opened his
Vatican to all the marvels of ancient art ? " But at last,
" at the Council of Trent, the Church examined herself.
She asked herself whether she had always done her duty
conscientiously ; and she promised herself to be more
strict with herself in future. Iconoclastic Protestantism
had condemned art ; the Church saved it ; but she
wished it to be without reproach " (534). With this
idea, men like Cardinal Paleotti came forward. They
fought the Protestants, but were compelled to fight them
on the ground not of imagination, but of reason and
common-sense. Molanus tries to explain how the
Christopher and Nicholas and George legends could have
grown up. " Thus, poesy recoils before good sense.
Unluckily, pure reason has never inspired artists ; and
henceforth there was no hope that the story of St. George
would ever give birth to a masterpiece. It is not only

the old popular Christianity of the Middle Ages which is condemned by the new spirit ; [Molanus condemns] also that pathetic Christianity which we may call Franciscan Christianity." And " this appeal to austerity was only too well heard. Strange to say, on this point the Renaissance conspired with the Church." For Molanus and his friends hated nudities, and the Renaissance had a taste for ample and elaborate drapery.

" Thus an age of decency and reason announced itself. After 1560, everything conspired to kill medieval art. With the miracle-plays, the iconographic traditions of the past began to disappear ; at the same moment the Church reviewed those traditions, discovered that most of them were stamped with the excessive credulity of past ages, and asked the artists to abandon them. Medieval art must needs succumb. Its charm was that it had kept the candour of childhood. This art resembled the medieval Church itself ; it resembled faith which does not discuss, but sings. Such an art could not even be touched with doubt. . . . The art of the Middle Ages, which was nothing but simple faith and spontaneity, could not survive that spirit of examination which owes its outburst to the Reformation. Henceforward there can be only one resource for the Christian artist ; to stand face to face with the Gospel and interpret it as he feels it. Thus will Rembrandt do, and thus will Poussin ; for, henceforward, Catholics will be no more supported by tradition than the Protestants themselves in this new age which begins at the Council of Trent ; the artist will now owe nothing to anyone but himself. So, from time to time, we shall have a few men in Europe capable of interpreting the Gospel in accordance with their temperament or their genius ; but there will be no longer, as in the Middle Ages, a collection of traditions respected everywhere and capable of raising the most moderate artist above himself. We shall still have Christian artists ; we shall no longer have a Christian art."

With these melancholy words Mâle closes his valuable book ; but let us look more closely into the facts and the inferences.

First, the iconography of the greatest age of Gothic art had owed comparatively little to the miracle-play. The main creators here, apart from the artists themselves, had been learned ecclesiastics here and there, such as Abbot Suger at St.-Denis, or Abbot Samson at St. Edmundsbury, or the authors of a good many surviving sets of verses which were composed as explicatory legends to be painted under some great series of pictures.[1] The influence of the miracle-play, so admirably traced by Mâle in that third volume, is, as he points out in its place, mainly late ; it belongs to an age when Gothic art was already running fast to seed ; it coincides, for instance, with the shopwork of the English alabaster factories. What effect need the disappearance of the miracle-play have had (to choose among the best-known and most obvious examples) upon the portals of Chartres, the serious quatrefoils on the west front of Amiens, or the sportive panels on the *portail des libraires* at Rouen ?

Secondly, it is historically incorrect to date this dissatisfaction with the medieval sacred drama from the Reformation. Here, as in so many other fields, the Reformers did no more than insist loudly, and often brutally, on things which pious and orthodox folk had murmured more discreetly for some time past, and in which satirists had long found theme for mockery. Chaucer shows no respect either for the tragedy or for the comedy of the religious drama ; either for Herod strutting on high or for the farce of Noah bringing his wife to ship. A contemporary of his, who may or may not have been a Lollard, but who certainly bases all his criticisms on religious and moral assumptions which most modern Christians would admit, is far more outspokenly critical of that drama. It had been invented (men had

[1] E.g. those published by Dr. M. R. James in Camb. Antiq. Soc., 8vo Series No. XXVIII, pp. 156 ff., and XXXVIII, pp. 13 ff.

pleaded in earlier days), to strengthen the faith of the
multitude ; yet to this author it is mainly objectionable
because the mixture of truth and fable, of edification
and folly, has resulted in a weakening of faith.[1]   An
extraordinarily interesting light comes to us from the
York records.[2]   In 1425 a Franciscan friar, William of
Melton, " Doctor of Divinity, and most famous preacher
of the Word of God, came to this city and in his various
sermons commended to the people the aforesaid play
[i.e. the elaborate series of Bible-plays which were performed from dawn to dark, each scene by a trade-gild
or a group of gilds, on Corpus Christi Day].   He affirmed
that the play, in itself, was good and most laudable.
Yet he said that the citizens of the said city, and other
foreigners who flowed in upon that holy-day, busy themselves greatly not only with the said holy-day pageant
but also in gluttony and drunkenness, shoutings and songs
and other insolences, paying no attention whatever
[minime attendentes] to the Church service appointed for
that day.   And, sad to say, they thus lose the indulgences
granted in that matter by Urban the Fourth of blessed
memory [a long list of indulgences for attendance in
church on Corpus Christi and following days].   And
therefore it seemed salutary to this friar William, and he
would fain bring the people of the city thereunto, that
the play should take place on one day and the Corpus
Christi procession on the next, so that folk might flock
to church on that holy-day and attend divine service for
the obtaining of these indulgences."   It was enacted,
therefore, that the pageants should thenceforward be
played on the eve of the feast.   But, as the editor tells
us, " the influence of Willelmus soon passed ; the people

[1] Compare the extracts from Robert Mannyng of Brunne, printed on
p. 402 of Social Life in Britain, and from a preacher of about 1400 in
Medieval Garner, p. 570, and in Life in Medieval Europe, p. 191.

[2] York Memorandum Book, vol. ii, Surtees Soc., 1914, pp. 124, 156–8 ;
cf. introd., pp. 46 ff.   The version of Friar Melton's action given in The
Cambridge Hist. of Eng. Lit. is strangely distorted.

obtained two holidays, but continued to perform their plays on Corpus Christi day and relegated the religious procession to the following day."

The second York incident was in 1431. The goldsmiths complained of the insupportable burden of having to produce two scenes of the play. " On the other hand, since the stonemasons of this city murmured among themselves concerning the pageant assigned to them in the Corpus Christi play, wherein Fergus was scourged, seeing that the matter of that pageant is not contained in Holy Scripture, and that it caused rather laughter and shouting than devotion, and sometimes quarrels and contentions and fights arose therefrom among the people, and that they could seldom or never perform and play that pageant by clear daylight, as the earlier pageants do, therefore the said masons desired greatly to be relieved of this their pageant, and to be assigned to some other which is in accordance with Holy Scripture, and which they can perform and play by daylight." [1]

The City Council sympathized with both the petitioning gilds, and transferred to the masons the pageant of Herod, which hitherto had been one of the two assigned to the goldsmiths.

Very nearly at this same time, St. Antonino was writing at Florence. He was not only a scholar and archbishop but also a man of remarkable practical insight and knowledge of the world. We find him complaining that, in general, " the [theatrical] representations of spiritual things which are made nowadays are mixed with

---

[1] The episode of Fergus (otherwise called Belzeray), resting upon the same sort of apocryphal foundation as that of Joachim and Anne, deals with a Jew who laid hands on the Virgin's bier, and whose hands clave to it by miracle. It is one of the scenes carved on the north side of Notre-Dame (figured in *Medieval Garner*, p. 701). The story is given fully in the *Golden Legend* (Assumption of B.V.M.), and it was one of those painted on the walls of Eton College Chapel for the instruction of those royal scholars. Since it dealt with the last scene of all, the Assumption, it was natural that dusk should come on before the masons were called upon for their performance.

many jests and buffooneries and masquerades." [1] And, a generation later, in 1469, we get a most significant glimpse of this theatre in an ordinary French village. The Archdeacon of Josas, in the Diocese of Paris, reported on his visit to St.-Vrain (Seine-et-Oise) : " Note, that the rural dean gave leave for playing the play of St. Sebastian on Our Lady's Day in September, and on the Sunday following. The players were Michel Datilli, Geoffroy Levain, Jean Bérault, Roger Cordier, and Pierre Jeudi, with Guillot Bardon, who dwelleth at Lèdeville, and Antoine Simonnet of Marolles. They rehearsed their play in the Chapel of St.-Vrain, denying God and fighting with each other." [2] A Hungarian friend tells me of a common proverb in that country, answering to the English slang : " A went for B bald-headed " ; it runs : " A went for B as Christ went for the shoemaker." This records a similar occasion, on which one performer taunted the other for his trade, and all dramatic proprieties were suddenly swept away by professional rivalry. It was quite natural, therefore, for any reforming saint to discourage the miracle-play ; and here St. Charles Borromeo, however he might shock the multitude, was creating no real religious breach but rather drawing an inevitable inference from saints of the past. In 1565 he, like the Parlement of Paris, prohibited the Passion Play : moreover, he forbade all theatrical representations on the Church holy-days. [3] Reformation and Counter-Reformation did indeed sweep much away ; but to describe the age which there ended as " the happy age of innocence " seems almost as bold as it would be to apply that same regretful phrase to French society

[1] *Summa Major*, pars. iii, tit. viii, c. 4, § 12.

[2] *Visites archidiaconales de Josas*, ed. Alliot, 1902, p. 336.

[3] Dejob, pp. 212–14. His severity against actors in general was such that the municipality of Milan protested formally to the Pope ; they complained that this puritanism " scandalized and shocked the innocent, and left the guilty no alternative but hypocrisy or despair." Yet in this St. Charles was following medieval Canon Law, and the sentiments of great medieval ecclesiastics.

before 1789. The world of 1500 had outgrown things that were often far from innocent, and no longer even happy. The reluctance of the York masons cannot have been an isolated incident.

So, again, with a great deal of the carved or painted things with which the mystery-play was bound up. When Mâle writes (p. 536) " a good half of the master-pieces which we admire in our churches were inspired by fables," we recognize this as true of later medieval art, and probably even of the thirteenth century. But can we recognize the same indisputable truth in the words with which he continues ?—" These legends had been more fruitful and beneficent than any history whatsoever, in the days when they were taken as authentic ; but those days were past." Is not this modern antiquary out of harmony, on that point, with all the best Christian thought ?   Great fathers like Origen had not known these legends ; even St. Gregory the Great, in the Dark Ages, had despised and ignored the fable of Constantine's leprosy ; Monsignor L. Duchesne pointed this out in his edition of the *Liber Pontificalis*. If, in the thirteenth century, Catholics believed implicitly in things which Gregory the Great had despised, and which no educated Catholic defends nowadays, this was not because the inventions were more fruitful and beneficent than the truth, but because men lacked certain methods of approach to truth which have been constructed by the labour and ingenuity and sincerity of twenty succeeding generations of mankind. It can scarcely be doubted that St. Bernard or Roger Bacon would have repudiated any sentimental hankering after what they had once recognized as fables, as vehemently as Luther or Calvin did. Their last word would not have been a regretful " but those days are past ! " but rather an energetic " let them pass, and God will give us better days in their stead ! "   " Instead of thy fathers thou shalt have children, whom thou mayest make princes in all the earth."

And such was the attitude of really great churchmen,

when once the Renaissance had begun to open men's minds to historical truth. Ludovicus Vives, the great Spanish humanist and educational reformer of the first half of the sixteenth century, had no hesitation in calling upon all straightforward minds to winnow boldly the chaff from the wheat. He wrote : " With what serious patience did the ancient Greeks and Romans seek the truth, and what pains they took to set it clearly forth ! " But the men who have come after them have almost entirely lost that factor of [accurate] memory and that of prudence. . . . Even in the books which are supposed to be Latin, such as the *De Vitis Philosophorum*, or the moralized *Gesta Romanorum*, what need was there of so great falsehoods ? Why could they not find the moral teaching which they sought in the real deeds of the Romans ? But let us suppose these things, grave as they are, to be within the bounds of toleration. What is it when this same licence of lying has crept into holy things, or rather has been openly borne into them ? For example, the traditional teaching concerning Constantine's leprosy and his bath in children's blood ; of the leprosy of Vespasian, of Gamaliel, of Berenice, the Acts of Christ and of the Blessed Virgin ? [1] We cry and bark at lesser things than this, and at these falsehoods we connive ; yet, if these come into the hands of impious folk, they turn our holiest and most earnest piety into a mockery fit to be hissed from the stage. Nor are we more religious in our traditions of things that stand nearer to us. [Each nation has its own false patriotic histories.] Nor do we keep truth more exactly when we write the lives of the saints ; though here all should have been exact and precise ; each has written their deeds according to his own affection for the man, so that the story is dictated

[1] These last two will be recognized as the already-mentioned apocryphal legends of Joachim and Anne and the Childhood of the Lord. The Leprosy of Constantine, a legend despised by St. Gregory, became in due time the foundation of Constantine's fictitious Donation to the Roman See, which was implicitly believed for nearly 700 years and upon which the medieval papal claims were to a great extent founded.

not by truth but by the writer's mood. How unworthy of saints and Christian men is that history of the saints which men call *Golden Legend* ? I know not wherefore it should be called golden, seeing that it is written by a man of iron mouth and leaden heart. What can we name that is baser than this book ? Oh, how shameful it is to us Christians that the most excellent deeds of our saints have not been handed down more truly and exactly, whether for the knowledge or for the imitation of their great virtue, seeing that the Greek and Roman authors took such care in writing of their own warriors and philosophers and sages ! " [1]

Again, Melchior Cano was one of the greatest among the bishops who sat on the Council of Trent.[2] In his *De Locis Theologicis*, written about 1550, when we come to the eleventh book, we find him insisting upon the impossibility of separating theology from history, and the consequent necessity of treating ecclesiastical traditions critically, though not, of course, with hypercriticism. The current story of Trajan freed from hell by the prayers of Pope Gregory, accepted implicitly by Dante and in another sense by the author of Piers Plowman, he rejects as a mere fable, and regrets that it had been believed " not by the multitude only, but even by St. Thomas [Aquinas] in his youth." Although, from Cyprian onwards, many Fathers have described the three Magi as kings, and this is therefore the reigning opinion, "yet this common tradition in the Church affords absolutely no proof [of its truth]." Again, though antiquity has consistently handed down the tradition that the Miracle of Cana took place on the anniversary of the Epiphany, yet " we can take no certain proof from the public commemoration of seasons." He knows that many cherished traditions are false; that the legend of the

---

[1] *De Causis Corrupt. Artium*, lib. ii *ad fin* ; *Opera*, Bâle, 1555, p. 371.

[2] Modern orthodox authorities like *The Catholic Encyclopædia* and the Freiburg *Kirchenlexikon* speak of his " imperishable name," " worthy of a place next St. Thomas Aquinas," " epoch-making work," etc., etc.

Eleven Thousand Virgins is absurd.; that "certainly
the story of St. Thomas the Apostle is an apocryphal
fiction, since not only has [Pope] Gelasius said this [in a
passage embodied in Canon Law] but Augustine also
[in more than one passage]." [1] He is well aware of the
weakness even of the early Church historians—Philo,
Sozomenus, Eusebius—" among ecclesiastics, there is not
one who can be taken as a thoroughly trustworthy
[*probabilis*] historian." Is there nothing trustworthy,
then, in past records ? Yes ; but only if we make proper
distinctions ; some are far more trustworthy than others ;
but in the least trustworthy class stand "edifying"
writers. Among the pagan Greeks and Romans, on the
other hand, " some, impelled either by love of truth or
by the shamefastness of native modesty, have so abhorred
lying that we ought perhaps to blush to find that certain
Gentile historians have been more veracious than our
own. I say it rather with grief than in contumely, that
[Diogenes] Laertius wrote the Lives of the Philosophers
far more strictly than Christians have written the Lives
of the Saints ; and that Suetonius has rehearsed the
affairs of the emperors with far more impartiality and
integrity than Catholics have rehearsed, I do not say the
story of the emperors, but [even] of martyrs, virgins and
confessors. For those ancient authors, when dealing with
good emperors or philosophers, do not suppress either
their faults or the suspicion of fault ; again, with the
wicked, they show even such colour of virtue as these had.
But very many of ours [*nostri plerique*] are either slaves
to partiality, or even deliberately invent so much that I
am not only ashamed but disgusted at them." Vives,
he continues, has very justly pilloried these men " who,
in the place of piety, have thought good to invent lies
for religion's sake " ; the net result is that even truths
are rendered dubious. " Such men sometimes paint us
the saints such as the saints themselves, though they

---

[1] This story of St. Thomas is among those which Mâle enumerates as
specially dear to medieval artists.

could have been, would have refused to be. For who
can believe that St. Francis, when the lice had been shaken
off, was wont to put them again upon himself "; or,
again, an equally absurd story about St. Dominic ?
The book *Vitaspatrum*, commonly ascribed to St. Jerome,
has very little in it that Jerome actually wrote. " Of the
same sort also is that foolish and barbarous book of the
Nativity of St. Mary " [i.e. of Joachim and Anne] " and
many other things which Erasmus has most diligently
and justly refuted. . . . Therefore the Church of Christ
is sadly incommoded by these men who think they cannot
excellently set forth the noble deeds of the saints unless
they trick them out with fictitious revelations and
miracles. Wherein human impudence hath spared
neither the holy Virgin nor Christ our Lord, but men
have done with their histories as with other saints,
allowing their frivolous human fancies to mingle therein
with many vain and ridiculous details. In former years,
when I was at the Council of Trent, I heard from some
that this evil was remedied by Aloysio Lippomano,
Bishop of Verona, who had published a History of the
Lives of the Saints after a uniform and serious method.
But I have not yet been able to see this, nor has any
other come into my hands which, to me at least, would
seem trustworthy. It will be a hard and burdensome task,
yet most profitable to all Christian folk, that someone
should now supply a work worthy of the Saints, of the
Church, and of Christ." Meanwhile, however, the
printing-press and the censorship are often responsible
for the popularity of gross errors. Cano knows of a
priest who " is fully convinced that there is no falsehood
whatsoever in anything that has once been printed," for
how can he believe that the authorities would not only
permit lies to be printed, but actually fortify them with
the privilege of exclusive copyright ? " The multitude
reads those books all the more incautiously, because it
sees them approved not only by the civil magistrates, but
even by those who are definitely appointed as censors of

doctrine in Christ's Church." The common herd demands religious fiction, and supply follows the demand. Moreover, these manufacturers of falsehood "imagine that they have the more liberty in this matter, since they see most famous authors taking it as a true rule of history to write those things which are vulgarly counted as true. Nor do I here excuse the author of the book called *Speculum Exemplorum*,[1] nor even of the history entitled *Golden Legend*. For in that book you will more often read monstrosities of miracles than real miracles ; for it was written by a man of iron mouth and leaden heart, and certainly of small gravity or prudence in mind." Even Vincent of Beauvais and St Antonino of Florence, in their laborious compilations, " have taken less trouble to relate true things and certainties, than to rake together every detail that they could find written in any booklet [*schedulis*] whatsoever."

Here, then, are facts which we have to consider side by side with what Mâle gives us. He quotes to us frankly and fully from Molanus ; but he seems not to suspect how much support Molanus could have claimed from like-minded predecessors in the Middle Ages, and from contemporaries in the Counter-Reformation. He writes sadly : " This cold-blooded little chapter of Molanus marks clearly the end of a chapter in human history." True ; but even in the history of art we must some-times look coldly at the facts ; nor do all our natural regrets for a vanished world excuse us from a careful and two-sided analysis of the causes. That early Protes-tantism was often hasty and bungling is admitted nowa-days by all reasonable and well-informed writers ; it is as much of a truism as the complementary fact that very serious corruptions sheltered under the wing of the

---

[1] Possibly the *Speculum Morale*, compiled as a complementary volume to the great encyclopædia of Vincent of Beauvais by an anonymous sub-contemporary ; or perhaps Herolt's *Promptuarium Exemplorum*, of which a translation by Mr. C. C. S. Bland will shortly be published by Routledge and Co.

Catholic Church. All men are now agreed that some change was then needed ; again, all are agreed that the surgery was often clumsy and ill-informed, and that, here and there, the changes created worse difficulties than they were designed to overcome. But, when we have said this, have we in fact said more than truth must allege against all surgeries, literal or metaphorical, in the light of four centuries of later experience ? Ambroise Paré was one of the great surgeons of all time, and he was roughly contemporary with Molanus and Cranmer. Would Paré have dealt with a case of appendicitis any more successfully than Cranmer dealt with the reform of the Liturgy ? Was any worse injustice done at the Reformation than by the orthodox emperors of early Christianity, who forcibly suppressed the schools of Athens, who made it penal for any man thenceforward to worship as the whole Empire had worshipped for centuries past, and who robbed the temples of a booty far exceeding all the spoils gathered by Henry VIII and the Protestant princes of Germany ? Let us ask ourselves therefore, as coolly as Molanus might ask himself in the light of modern knowledge, what was the alternative which would have saved medieval art ? Suppose that no Lollard or Lutheran or Calvinist had ever existed ; suppose that the sores of the Church had been left entirely in the hands of practitioners like the Fathers of the Council of Trent ; suppose these to have been unsoured and unjostled, doing their tranquil and reflective best without any heretics to shake their nerves ; what then would have happened to the painter and the sculptor ?

What was to be done with that " good half " of subjects which had inspired the best of Gothic art, and which were in fact fabulous ? Long before Luther, the Renaissance had begun to open men's eyes here. That fable of Constantine's leprosy, for instance, was exploded almost simultaneously by the humanist Lorenzo Valla in Italy and by Cardinal Nicholas of Cues in Germany. How was the new light to be concealed from the ordinary

educated man, from the merchant, for instance, like
Ralph Hythlodaye, whom More takes for the narrator
of his Utopia ?   How could it be permanently concealed
from these men that the whole story of Joachim and
the Nativity of the Virgin Mary was fabulous, and that,
as Cano saw, there was no real certitude in the fact that
events of this kind had been attached by immemorial
tradition to certain days of the year ?   And, if the merchant might learn the truth, why not the artisan and
even the peasant ?   Would our imaginary perfect reformers
have condescended to that policy of the modern *Action
Française* ?   Would they have held that the uneducated
must be encouraged to accept dogmas which his educated
director believes to be false ?   Will the historian of four
centuries hence be more impressed by the Reformers who
cut out certain acknowledged fables, or by the Anglican
bishops who have retained St. Anne (with added emphasis)
and St. Catharine of Alexandria in their Revised Liturgy,
though there are at least two ecclesiastical historians on
the bench ?   Mâle does not suggest that the *Golden Legend*
could possibly have maintained its sway throughout this
new age of enlightenment ; except, of course, in the
sense in which Cinderella and Balder, Atalanta and
Theseus will always live on.   It must go, then, but how
must it go ?   All the medieval heresies, or nearly all, had
demanded sharp surgery here.   Lollards had died for
their belief, shared by orthodox pietists like the author
of *Dives and Pauper*, that these unrealities led men into
actual idolatry.   The best of them were guided by moral
principles which were latent in the highest art of the
thirteenth century itself.   They did not stand alone in
the conviction that, for religion's sake, art must now be
brought back more closely to truth and to everyday
morality ; these heretics differed from the most earnest
men among the orthodox mainly in their resolve to
grapple themselves with a problem from which the
authorities persistently shrank.   Was it the fault of those
who tried to moralize religious art, if that art had drifted

so far from morality that the operation must prove fatal ? When a surgeon, removing the morbid tissue, finds that he has extinguished all that was left of life, do we fairly describe him as the slayer of his patient ? We cannot justly judge the Reformers without bearing constantly in mind that the Tridentine Fathers practically admitted the necessity of much of this surgery ; " the Church reviewed those traditions, discovered that most of them were stamped with the excessive credulity of past ages, and asked the artists to abandon them." We need not enter here again into the question of image-worship in general ; we are dealing with the image simply in so far as it is bound up with medieval artistic traditions ; and, on this point, we find that Trent agrees in the main with Protestantism. How, then, can it be seriously contended that it was Protestantism which killed medieval symbolic art ? The Renaissance, more than a century before Luther, had begun to show that a good half of this art reposed upon legends which would not bear examination. The Council of Trent, after Luther, recognised this fact, and practically proscribed a great deal of medieval iconography. The average Catholic dignitary of the seventeenth century had less sympathy with Gothic statuary than high Anglicans like Andrewes and Cosin and Laud.

The Renaissance had been steadily putting these legends, one by one, into a prison in which they must needs die of cold and starvation. Popes and cardinals, in later days, confessed that these legends deserved to die. In the meanwhile, a revolutionary mob (to picture Protestantism at its worst) had burst into the prison and cut the prisoners' throats. Therefore, even if we confine ourselves, as hitherto, to the purely theological side of the question, must we not decide that the slayers were more truly those who made it impossible for the legends to live, and whose descendants approved of the death, than those who hastened this end by rough methods which the others would have repudiated ?

Even if we were dealing with Protestant countries only, justice would compel us to take these things into account. But we are concerned also with that half of Europe which remained Catholic, and which has generally been more active in the pursuit of art than any Protestant land. How could the Reformation have killed Gothic art in France and Italy and Spain, if it had really been vigorous in those lands ? The religious revolution has done practically nothing to affect image-worship in those countries, because image-worship corresponds to a deep and imperious instinct in a multitude of hearts. If the medieval symbolism, and all those other characteristics which distinguish Gothic from Classical or Renaissance, had been half so deeply rooted, how could that art, almost within a single generation, have withered more hopelessly in France and Spain and Italy than in England ? Does not the root of all misconception in this matter lie here, that modern critics often imagine a closer nexus between special forms of art and special religious denominations than has ever existed in fact ? I deliberately choose here the word *denomination* rather than *faith*, because I have given evidence elsewhere for the conviction that the fundamental faith or unfaith of the medieval multitude differed far less from that of the modern multitude than is commonly supposed, and that an intensive study of medieval life, by students of all schools, will make this increasingly evident.

CHAPTER XX

PROTESTANTISM AND ART

I MUST use the term Protestantism, in this chapter, in its most ordinary sense, as applying to all the churches which, in the sixteenth century, cast off the Roman obedience. This definition is in accord not only with the sense in which many generations have been accustomed to understand the word, but also with its obvious etymology. All Anglo-Catholics, for instance, are in a position of protest against certain essential Roman Catholic claims ; in some cases, it is perhaps that protest alone which distinguishes them from Roman Catholics. Medieval art, on the other hand, was unquestionably produced by people who accepted those claims in a sense in which even the extremest Anglo-Catholic does not ; and if it be true, as Mâle argues and as many believe, that medieval art was the exact expression of medieval religion, then Mâle is plainly right in dividing as he does, between Protestant and Roman Catholic ; and those who, like myself, are inclined seriously to question his conclusion, are yet bound to follow in the line of his arguments. But we must bear in mind what he seems sometimes to forget, that this division, like all other things in this actual world, is less absolute in fact than in logic, and especially that, in England, the Elizabethan settlement was designedly vague enough to leave room for a very great deal of what is now called Anglo-Catholicism inside the prevailing Protestantism. The most extreme of Anglican Protestants is accustomed, in the Creed, to assert his belief in the Catholic Church. Protestantism, therefore, covers a number of religious bodies, in many cases widely divergent, of which the

Anglican Church is on the whole the most conservative. And we may ask : " Is there anything in the general theory of Protestantism, reasonably interpreted, that is necessarily fatal to medieval art as a whole, apart, that is, from such details as have been condemned or discouraged by enlightened Roman Catholics themselves ? Or, if not in theory, has Protestantism in practice been such that medieval art could not live with it ?

The subject has already been discussed more than once at some length. Readers who are especially interested in it should refer to the debate between Messrs. Eugène Müntz and N. Weiss in the *Revue des Revues* for March 1 and July 15, 1900, and in the *Bulletin de la Société du protestantisme français* for October 15, 1900 ; also to Mr. Joseph Crouch's *Puritanism and Art*.[1] The French articles, as the less accessible, ought to occupy us most here. Weiss being a Protestant pastor, and Müntz an art-historian apparently holding liberal Catholic views, they naturally differed on a good many points. Müntz was evidently less familiar with his patristic authorities and his Church history than with art matters proper ; Weiss, again, is principally concerned to defend his own co-religionists, and does so with some heat ; but I will attempt to put down nothing here which is not either agreed between the two disputants, or vouched with good evidence by one or other of them.

As there are many forms of Protestantism, so there have been many degrees of friendliness or enmity to art. Calvin, on the whole, was the least friendly in theory, and his followers have been the most inartistic in practice. Yet even Calvin was far less definitely inimical to art than is generally imagined. Like Luther, he recognized it as one of God's gifts. In his *Institution*, which sums up his whole doctrine, he writes : " Yet am I not so scrupulous as to judge that no images should be endured or suffered ; but, seeing that the art of painting and carving images cometh from God, I require that the

[1] Cassell and Co., 1910. See Appendix 30.

practice of art should be kept pure and lawful. . . . Therefore men should not paint nor carve any thing but such as can be seen with the eye ; so that God's Majesty, which is too exalted for human sight, may not be corrupted by fantasies which have no true agreement therewith."[1]

Luther went a great deal farther. " I do not hold that the Gospel should destroy all the arts, as certain superstitious folk believe. On the contrary, I would fain see all arts, and especially that of music, serving Him who hath created them and given them unto us. . . . The Law of Moses forbade only the image of God ; the crucifix is not forbidden." He would have church walls painted with the Creation, Noah building his ark, etc. ; he thought all lords ought to paint the walls of their mansions with Bible scenes.

In practice, again, Luther corresponded with Dürer and was a warm friend and patron to Lucas Cranach. " One of the first specimens of Lutheran art was the reredos at Montbéliard, executed by Hans Leonhard Schaufelein and the ' Master of Messkirch,' which is now at the Museum of Vienna. This picture contains no less than 157 subjects, borrowed with one or two exceptions from the Gospels, and accompanied by long legends in German. Many parables will be noticed in it, a field rarely exploited by Catholic art. It was painted after 1526. . . . It was only at a later date that the principality became iconoclastic, under the influence of the reformers from French Switzerland." Again, " Long after Cranach's death, Lutheran churches continued to receive paintings."[2] They were mostly second-rate ; but they showed that Protestantism as such had no theory of destruction for religious art. Nor were they always second-rate ; among early Protestants we may name some really great artists ; Holbein, Dürer, Jean Goujon, and Bernard Palissy, who worked indiscrimi-

[1] *Instit.*, bk. i, c. xi, § 12.

[2] Müntz, pp. 490, 491.

nately for Protestant and Catholic patrons.[1] True, these
men had mostly learned their art in Catholic surroundings ; yet their very existence may keep us from drawing
too hard a line of division between the two creeds.
Müntz, who rehearses these and others, adds, " Such
names authorize us to assert that the Reformation, as
formulated by Luther, was by no means exclusive of
art." We must not, however, attempt to dispute the
general fact, that Protestantism was less favourable to
art in churches than was the Catholicism of that time,
and of a thousand preceding years. But, at its strictest,
it was less unfavourable than the earliest Christian
orthodoxy had often been ; and we must remember,
again, that even Lutheranism and Calvinism combined
did not control a full half of Europe. There was nothing,
therefore, to hinder a strong Catholic reaction ; if
thirteenth century art had really been a vital and growing thing in 1500, there was nothing in the mere existence
of Protestantism to prevent the orthodox half of Europe
from continuing, or if possible improving upon, the
medieval traditions. What really rendered this impossible was partly the fact that the movement had run its
natural course, and partly that great and pious Roman
theologians often condemned, or at least discouraged,
many of the things to which Protestantism was inimical,
and that the general public also looked upon the old
traditions as somewhat outworn. The orthodox masons
of York come as really into this problem as the unorthodox
iconoclasts.

But it remains for us to look more closely into Protestant practice during the first century of the Reformation.
Here, again, the harm wrought by revolutionaries is
sufficiently notorious, and it is a fact which must be taken
full account of at every point. Although, as we have

---

[1] Dürer never officially broke with Catholicism, but his letters and
diaries contain, as Müntz says, " regular professions of Lutheran faith."
Holbein was perhaps rather a sceptic than an acknowledged Protestant ;
but certainly he was not orthodox.

seen, much that was then destroyed was also condemned or discouraged by the Council of Trent, yet undoubtedly there was a great deal of vandalism among objects that were dogmatically innocuous, or that had lost much of their dogmatic significance with the progress of time. Here again, however, it is necessary to guard against the exaggeration of ignorance and cheap rhetoric. When we read that, " through the destruction of the monasteries by Henry's cut-throats . . . most of the very noblest examples of Gothic in England have utterly perished from the earth,"[1] it is as well to turn from this to the able and zealous Catholic Montalembert, who knew England very well, and who noted regretfully that " if we wish to form an idea of the majestic grandeur of monastic buildings, we must visit England. The work of devastation has been less complete and irreparable there than elsewhere."[2] On this point of Protestant vandalism, Weiss has no difficulty in convicting even Müntz of unjustifiable exaggeration. Both authors agree in emphasizing Zwingli's attitude in Switzerland.[3] Radical as this reformer was in many of his ideas, he was far from a complete iconoclast. He had great admiration for ancient art : " I yield to no man in admiration for pictures and statues," so long as they were not worshipped. Therefore he expressly protected the stained glass, since it led to no risk of idolatry.[4] With regard to the rest, he wrote a diatribe against images, and at his instigation the Zürich magistrates proclaimed that, in each parish where the majority should so decide, all images that were an object of worship should be removed and destroyed. The result was a very considerable destruction.

Calvin, on the other hand, protested more generally

---

[1] R. A. Cram, *The Gothic Quest*, p. 125.

[2] *Moines d'Occident*, l. xviii, ch. v (ed. 1882, vol. vi, p. 247).

[3] Pp. 484, 511 respectively.

[4] In incidental agreement with the author of *The Tale of Beryn*, who, as I have pointed out in an earlier chapter, represents his fifteenth century pilgrims as indifferent to the religious meaning of the windows.

against images : " I know the common proverb, that images are the books of unlettered folk, and that St. Gregory hath thus spoken : but the Spirit of God hath judged otherwise ; " i.e. Jeremiah x. 3, and Habakkuk ii. 18. He was persuaded that, under the Reformation, all folk would learn to read ; and in any case " all that men learn of God through images is frivolous and even abusive."[1] Later, in the same book, however, he writes less strongly, in the passage I have already quoted earlier in this chapter. This was in 1535 ; in 1562 civil wars in France led to a great deal of image-breaking, and Calvin pronounced definitely against this. God, he wrote, has not commanded us to destroy idols except in our own houses ; and he condemned the Protestant image-breakers of Lyons. Nor, even among the rank and file of the Huguenots, was iconoclasm ever " the rule," as Müntz asserts. Weiss shows that it was mainly confined to one brief period, in the fury of civil war (1562) ; and in the later phases of the struggle, destruction was mainly military, and was not confined to one side only ; at Dijon and Chartres, for instance, the Catholic leaders melted down Church plate and ornaments as Charles I did the plate of the Oxford colleges. And he quotes an orthodox writer of the time who confesses how, at Orléans, " the [Huguenot] lords and ministers took a good attitude, and showed that they approved not such abominations. . . . Proclamation was made to do no damage to the churches, nor to scratch a single image."[2]

Still less can we speak of systematic destruction in Germany as a whole. When Luther's former ally Carlstadt broke images and glass at Wittenberg (1521), Luther came out from his hiding-place at the Wartburg

---

[1] *Instit.*, bk. i, ch. xi, § 5.

[2] Weiss, p. 516, cf. p. 514 *note*, where he points out that, of all the 500 and more condemnations pronounced against Huguenots by the Parlement of Paris between 1547 and 1550, one only is against an act of iconoclasm.

to protest. Next year he preached openly against Carlstadt : we are free to possess images or not ; only, for
fear of abuse, it is better to have none.

Let us therefore avoid as much as possible this emphasis upon differences which, after all, are sometimes
artificial. As Catholicism and Protestantism profess alike
to have one and the same ultimate aim, so in fact, when
we take each at its best, the fundamental common factors
far outweigh the divergent details. It may often be
necessary to give these details far more than their face
value ; so long as one side or the other insists upon them
as principles, they must be treated as principles in general
discussion. St. Paul was seldom more in earnest, or
more persistent, than when he discussed circumcision
with St. Peter. But, while details thus force their
importance inexorably upon us, we must never so treat
them as to lose sight of deeper principles. We must
discuss side-issues so as to show their relative unimportance,
not so as to give them an artificial value.

A great deal of what is commonly written about
medieval architecture seems thus to put the cart before
the horse. It seems to rest upon two vicious assumptions, one demonstrably false and the other unprovable,
if not improbable.

First, that our Gothic cathedrals are the natural and
inevitable expression, in stone, of the Christian faith,
and of one special form of that faith, the Roman Catholic.
A priori, this theory is not without a certain specious
verisimilitude. If we chose to argue merely from our
own emotions in face of the statued porches or the solemn
altar-services, then those who regard these things as the
inevitable expression of the highest Christianity would
have as much right to their conviction as (for instance)
Renan had for the opposite feeling, that the Parthenon
was a more elevating work of art than Amiens. But we
have not here a question of feeling and taste alone ; it
is even more directly a question of history and experience.
If Amiens Cathedral were indeed the Roman Catholic

faith crystallized into stone, then the popes would have
been the first to foster Gothic art, and the last to let it
go ; indeed, why should they, under any conditions,
ever abandon that expression, any more than other
natural expressions, of the Catholic faith ? Yet, as a
matter of history, we may say with literal truth : The
nearer to Rome, the farther from Gothic ![1] Even if it
be an exaggeration to assert, with at least one responsible
writer, that only one Gothic church was built in Rome ;
yet it is unquestionable that no medieval city of comparable size and importance showed anything approaching the same indifference to, or even dislike for, Gothic.
Roughly speaking, the nearest examples here are the
cities nearest to Rome, which lay most definitely under
the papal eye, if not directly under papal government,
during the whole Gothic period. Venice had much Gothic
of an Arab cast ; and Venice was one of the least papal of
cities in Italy ; later, under Fra Paolo, she came near to
asserting actual independence. The builder of the great
Gothic basilica at Assisi, Frate Elia, did in his later years
actually repudiate papal authority and join the Emperor
Frederick II. Florence has a good deal of semi-Gothic
work, and Florence in the fourteenth century was in rebel-
lion against the popes, who not only excommunicated her
but adjudged her citizens to slavery. In France and in
Germany, again, the least Gothic districts are those
nearest to the Italian frontier, or to the great trade-
routes from Italy. Moreover, from the first moment
of the great papal revival onwards, when the popes rose
victorious from their struggle against the constitu-
tionalists at Constance and Bâle, they set their faces

[1] Lord Braye, in his recent reminiscences, praises his beloved Catholic
college of Prior Park for its " eighteenth century plan of magnificent
rectitude in design," in which he finds a congruity with the genius both
of the Latin liturgy and of the imperial Roman Church, and which he
contrasts most favourably with " the Pugin-Ruskin school " (*Times Lit.
Sup.*, July 28, 1927, p. 515). Many will agree with him even as a matter
of taste ; but in the present connexion the one thing that matters is the
historical fact.

more definitely against Gothic architecture than the English Protestants. If, as might well happen, some pope were elected in our own day who was entirely ignorant of Gothic art, and if he were suddenly kindled to enthusiasm by such volumes as those of Émile Mâle, he would have to end his days in ignorance of all that could not be picked up from books and photographs ; his knowledge of this particular subject would necessarily be the second-hand knowledge of (for instance) an American too busy or too poor to travel in Europe. Indeed, the American might well have an advantage here ; for it is possible that some American town no larger than Rome may possess a really good piece of modern Gothic ; Boston, for instance, is building or has built a small memorial church which shows an understanding of the Gothic forms which could hardly be found in Rome. Not only geographically, but aesthetically, the splendid English minsters of the Middle Ages are farther from Rome than Rome is from Constantinople. Again, not only does a detached modern critic like Remi de Gourmont expose the impossibility of those theories which may be said to culminate in Huysmans, but some thoroughly orthodox art-lovers have at all times raised their voices against it. At Abbeville, at Amiens, scholars might be found repudiating it two generations ago, when it was in the bloom of early youth.[1] " We must drop the term *Christian Art*, and recognize that Gothic speaks no more to the soul than other styles, unless it be to the souls of Catholics who insist on finding symbolism where none exists and nobody has ever thought of putting it. . . . We might say of the medieval architects, as of the ancient authors, that, if they came back to life, they would often be greatly astonished at the ideas which we attribute to them." The first of these sentences is significant even in its exaggeration ; the second is not even exaggerated.

[1] *Mém. Soc. d'Émulation d'Abbeville*, 1852, pp. 747 ff., 761-2 ; *Bull. Soc. Ant. de Picardie*, 1846, pp. 324 ff.

There is far more historic, as well as æsthetic, probability in deriving Gothic art from the traditions of the
half-nomad northerners who hunted, and reared cattle,
and tilled scanty patches of corn amid primeval forests
where the pines and beeches run up to eighty feet before
they throw out their first branches. Prof. Lethaby
quotes many such suggestions on pp. 87–90 of *The Legacy
of the Middle Ages* (Oxford, 1926) ; and he himself sums
up : " Our last sight of Gothic before it disappeared is
a fringe of much crocketed pinnacles like pine-trees
ranged along a peaked horizon. The northern forests
had nurtured a people who could do no other than
build according to their ideals ; not knowing but only
doing. As the Greek expressed lucidity and serenity,
so northern art had the mystery of the great forests
behind it."

Moreover, it is significant that the apostles of that
other theory—Huysmans and his followers—have been
men whose general outlook on life would have appealed
far less to any of the great saints or philosophers or
moralists of the Middle Ages, than to the average Thor-
worshipper of the German forests, or to the freethinker
of Renaissance Rome. Is it indeed worth while to make
a single proselyte at the cost of such theories as these ?
Is it not far more honourable to human nature, and at
the same time far more consonant with obvious facts,
to conclude that the purely religious element in Gothic
is that which appeals not only to all religious minds, of
whatever creed, but also to every truly religious chord
in what may be, predominantly, an irreligious mind ?
I do not say, of course, that the appeal is equal in every
case ; but only that the differences are dependent far
more on artistic than on religious temperament. Among
Romans or Southern Italians, only a minority truly
appreciate the greatest French Gothic. On the other
hand, we may well doubt whether Huysmans ever felt
it in every fibre of his being, or drank it in with such
physical enjoyment, as the Protestant Ruskin who ended

in something like Agnosticism, and William Morris who had no use whatever for organized religion.

The second assumption is complementary to the first. Not only (we are told) did Roman Catholicism in fact create Gothic art, but no other spirit could by any possibility have created it. Here, of course, we have a theory immune against all attack from the ground of plain historical fact; speculations as to what might have happened are as secure from absolute disproof as they are wanting in conclusive proof. But we have a right to judge them by this principle of medieval philosophy : *Quod gratis asseritur, gratis negatur* ; if a man brings no sufficient reasons for his assertions, neither do I need formal reasons for my disbelief. Let us suppose for a moment that, instead of Christianity conquering the polytheism of the barbarian invaders, the religious victory had gone the other way. With the help of pagan classical literature and art and institutions (of which we may reasonably suppose these polytheists to make use, and perhaps even as freely as the Catholic Church did) they would gradually have settled down from the turmoil of the Dark Ages into long medieval centuries, during which commerce and culture would rapidly develop ; and, until commerce had reached its full modern development in the banking system, the most obvious form of investment would have been in building. So far the hypothesis would seem entirely reasonable ; it is very much the story of Arabic culture. These men would have built more and more ambitiously ; why not, then, as high as a Gothic cathedral ? Italian churches never ran so high in the Middle Ages, nor did those of Southern France ; it was not religion that created this aspiring height ; it was something in the northern mind and in northern experience. Is it a mere chance that those forests of pillars, branching into vault-ribs high overhead, were characteristic of populations familiar with taller and thicker forests than the south ever produced in those centuries ? It is at least far more probable that the contrast between Amiens and San Francesco at Assisi (which might easily be greatly increased by choosing two other examples) is due rather to such considerable differences of social or business outlook and environment as we know to have existed between north and south, than to the almost negligible religious differences between the mind of a Picard and an Umbrian in the thirteenth century. Is not the romance element in Gothic even greater than the Christian ?

In detail of ornament, there is no reason why this architecture of the supposed northern polytheists should have differed much from the Gothic that we know. They, also, would have copied the Saracen and Persian brocades that they bought, and Byzantine imagery and scroll-work, and those intricate patterns that the Celts loved, but had not invented, and the ruder patterns on the Viking ships. They too would have taken Constantinople by storm, and carried back with them not only classical Greek statues but, more valuable still, Greek ideas in art. There would seem no reason why their temples should not have been as full of gods and demi-gods and heroes as Chartres is of saints.

SOLOMON AT REIMS.

Charles the Great, whose ideas here as elsewhere ran before his time, counselled the representation of heroes as well as of saints. If our hypothetical artists had filled the windows with warriors, why should those figures have been less artistically effective than the famous De Montfort medallion at Chartres, or those De Clares in the choir windows of

Tewkesbury ? Their funeral effigies might have been practically identical with many of the best that we have in Europe ; and the statues of kings or queens or heroes round their portals might, in many cases, have been indistinguishable from those of Chartres. Or take, again, that figure from Reims of which Viollet-le-Duc kept a cast in his studio, and enjoyed the questions of his classical friends : " What is this Greek statue that I have never seen before ? " It is commonly called Solomon ; but by general confession there is no certainty in the attribution ; who would dare to say that it has anything so distinctly Christian in figure or in face that it could not have been fashioned to represent Ulysses himself, or that Viking Ulysses who first discovered America ? The main principles of Gothic art are to be found rather in construction than in detail.[1] Those piles of wall and buttress and tower, massed in alternate light and shade, sometimes frowning but mainly content to impose by their majesty of height and skyline, might as fitly commemorate some line of earthly kings, flanked by their warriors and ministers, as Christ with His royal ancestors and His saints. In one sense, the two motives may be a whole horizon apart ; they may be as different as sunset is from sunrise. But that is not to the present point ; in a Claude or a Turner, who will undertake to tell us with certainty whether the sun is rising or setting ? Would two intelligent visitors from Mars, standing far enough from the façade of Wells to grasp the whole general effect, necessarily agree with each other as to the heavenly or the earthly character of figures and canopies which both would admire as artistically effective ? Therefore, if polytheism had won that victory which I have taken the liberty of suggesting, would not the zealous polytheist of to-day, the Huysmans with his disciples, be

---

[1] For Ruskin's estimate of the value of mass and projection, and of those effects which are more likely to be suggested by natural scenery than by dogmatic religion, see the extract from *Seven Lamps of Architecture* (ch. iii, § 23–4) which I give in Appendix 31.

insisting to us that here is the one supreme inimitable art, built upon the glorious creed of Thor and Odin, and crowned with an æsthetic success to which no other creed could conceivably have attained ?

True, all this refers only to the general constructive and decorative principles of Gothic, and takes no account of the spiritual expression in such a group, for instance, as the Annunciation at Reims. There indeed, and in the Beau Dieu d'Amiens, and in a thousand Mary and Child groups, we have something as distinctive of Christianity, and sometimes of Catholic Christianity alone, as the great Buddha statues are of Buddhism, borrowed though they originally were from Greek models. But, among all these, it is only the Mary and Child that we may think of as normal in the ordinary village church; and villagers formed in those days the overwhelming majority of the population. No doubt there is often considerable grace of line even in the most rapid village daub; but this

LE BEAU DIEU D'AMIENS.

did not appeal to the worshipper as it appeals to the modern artist. Otherwise we cannot account for the fact, acknowledged by so earnest a modern Catholic as Maurice de Wulf, that Catholics as well as Protestants came to despise Gothic art.[1] Ruskin scarcely exaggerated when he wrote : " Observe, the change of which I speak has nothing whatever to do with the Reformation, or with any of its effects. It is a far broader thing than the Reformation. It is a change which has taken place not only in reformed England and reformed Scotland, but

[1] *Philos. and Civil. in the Middle Ages*, 1922, p. 8.

in unreformed France, in unreformed Italy, in unreformed Austria."[1] Dejob, again, emphasizes very truly
the remarkable neglect of the finest medieval art by these
orthodox art-writers of the Counter-Reformation. " Ver
Meulen, though he knows the works of the old masters,
does not seem touched by the faith which breathes from
most of them. As to [Cardinal] Paleotti and the other
Italian theorists, they scarcely make passing mention of
the primitives. . . . Shortly afterwards, these precursors,
in whose name men have attacked Raphael in our own
day, fell into an oblivion comparable to that into which
our medieval literature fell about the same time ; but a
much more surprising oblivion, since men had only to
open their eyes to see the works of the ancient masters,
whereas our *Chansons de Geste* had, so to speak, disappeared."[2]

But, while expressing my belief that a great deal of
the most popular writing on this subject has not only
ignored historical facts but has shown a want of serious
thought, let me not seem to exaggerate in the other
direction. A religious creed, and the buildings and
ornaments wrought by the men of that creed, may be
as closely related as soul and body ; I would not quarrel
with the metaphor, though it seems to me to partake of
exaggeration. Yet it is very hazardous to insist too much
on the relation even of soul and body. The story of
Socrates and the professional physiognomist is proverbial ;
if, again, we possessed no signed bust of any Roman
emperor, and had to identify the faces from what we
know of their histories, what disputes would there not be
among learned and unlearned ! and how few would be
found to have named even the twelve Cæsars aright !
In the light of such considerations, let us beware of too
hasty identifications between art and religious dogma.
What differentiates Lincoln Cathedral, in its present
Protestant hands, from Amiens is indeed mainly peculiar

[1] *Lect. Arch. and Painting*, IV, § 115 (Library ed., vol. xii, p. 139).
[2] P. 251.

to the Roman Catholic faith ; yet the far greater artistic differences between Amiens and St. Peter's at Rome are not denominational.

This does not mean that there were not many artists who felt religious inspiration while they worked, or that there are not far more worshippers now who from those works derive religious inspiration. It leaves us free to love Gothic art, to worship Gothic art if we will, but not to worship it in the name of one creed and to the exclusion of all others. Here, as everywhere else, those feel truest and deepest who do not entirely ignore that other men's deepest feelings may also be true.

CHAPTER XXI

THE ROOTS OF THE RENAISSANCE

HERE, then, we must again make an effort to clear our minds, and not to assume a closer connexion between the art and the religion of any period than the facts will warrant. That connexion was exceptionally close in the early thirteenth century; yet, even for that period, it is generally exaggerated. Here, for instance, let us turn again to a modern writer who is eminently suitable to illustrate my point. Why, asks Mr. Cram, has America lost the artistic spirit? And he continues : " Were the answer to this sought seriously ... we should find that all the Christian art that exists, whether it be architecture, sculpture, painting, music, craftsmanship, owes its life and its glory to one power, the Catholic Church, and we should find also that, although Protestantism has held dominion in Germany, England, Scandinavia, and the United States for several hundred years, it has produced no vital art of any kind ; such sporadic instances as have occurred possessing no connexion whatever with the dominant form of theology. We should also find that the decadence of art has been almost unbroken since the period called the Reformation. I argue nothing from these facts, I wish only to call attention to them."[1] These words are no unfair sample of the sort of writing which, because it flatters strong sectarian prejudices, is sure of success within a fairly wide circle, and, through its boldness of assertion, even outside the fold. This confident appeal to history is backed up neither here nor elsewhere by any shred of tangible historical evidence ; the facts from which Mr. Cram will

[1] *The Gothic Quest*, p. 85.

not argue, but upon which he will composedly take his stand and lift up his voice to command our attention, are simply exploded fictions. The whole passage is thoroughly typical of a whole school which descends ultimately from Ruskin, but which, substituting rhetoric for thought at every fresh step, and having by this time become separated from its living source by two or three generations of commonplace writers, lives now upon Ruskin's exaggerations and has forgotten that great man's qualifications. Here, for instance, is what Ruskin himself wrote (*Stones of Venice*, iv, § 53) : " There being no beauty in our recent architecture, and much in the remains of the past, and these remains being almost exclusively ecclesiastical, the High Church and Romanist parties have not been slow in availing themselves of the natural instincts which were deprived of all food except from this source ; and have willingly promulgated the theory, that because all the good architecture that is now left is expressive of High Church or Romanist doctrines, all good architecture ever has been and must be so—a piece of absurdity from which, though here and there a country clergyman may innocently believe it, I hope the common sense of the nation will soon manfully quit itself. It needs but little inquiry into the spirit of the past, to ascertain what, once for all, I would desire here clearly and forcibly to assert, that wherever Christian Church architecture has been good and lovely, it has been merely the perfect development of the common dwelling-house architecture of the period ; that, when the pointed arch was used in the street, it was used in the Church." And, elsewhere, Ruskin points out the notorious fact that Gothic art was even more despised in Roman Catholic countries, from the sixteenth century to almost the present day, than in Protestant countries. Nowhere are the churches more inartistic to-day than in Tyrol, which has been untouched by the Reformation.

Therefore, in correction of modern pleas which, on the face of them, seem grossly exaggerated, and which certainly have as yet made no pretence of adequate documentary vouchers, let us here follow very briefly the course of the Renaissance, and mark its actual effects upon art. For much of this present chapter which is not merely common knowledge, I have given documentary evidence elsewhere ; the rest will be supplied here.

The movement which we call Renaissance can be traced back very far indeed. In one very real sense, it began at least as early as the Norman Conquest of England; at that period came a great revival of art and letters, and therefore of thought, both orthodox and unorthodox. Side by side with Lanfranc and Anselm were Berengar of Tours, who anticipated some of Luther's work, and many little-known thinkers who harked back to those ancient Gnostics, the rationalizers of early religion.[1]   A century later, there came in simultaneously the complete Aristotle, upon which Aquinas and the other schoolmen based so much of Christian philosophy, and the Arab Averroes with a philosophy that was fundamentally and irreconcilably anti-Christian. The number of condemnations which have survived, from Paris and elsewhere, suffice to prove that there was, under the surface, a strong current of University thought no more friendly to orthodox Catholicism than the average University thought of to-day. Petrarch complained that, in Venice, orthodox Christian philosophy was laughed at as a " back number " ; Padua was a hotbed of Averroism ; and Marsilius of Padua, with the Englishman Ockham, worked out theories of Church and State which practically reduced the Pope himself to a mere figure-head. Petrarch, with his pupil Boccaccio, began to revive the serious study of classical antiquity ; Rienzo based his revolution in Rome upon ancient pagan precedent. Therefore this classical revival, even if we date it only from Petrarch, is a whole generation older than Lollardy,

[1] This was admirably brought out in a paper read by Prof. Alphandéry before the recent *Congrès d'Histoire du Christianisme* at Paris, which will be printed in the official report of that Congress.

just as Valla and Cusanus began systematically to destroy
medieval legend by the solvent of historical research
nearly a century before Luther's revolt.   Vives and
Melchior Cano derive from Valla and Cusanus ; therefore, even though no heretic had ever existed, orthodoxy
must have discovered, sooner or later, that there was one
only too real sense in which the Golden Legend must be
called the Legend of Lead.

Moreover, popes themselves at last began to lead the
way in this direction.   When, with the final failure of
the Council of Bâle (1443) the papacy emerged more
despotic than before, then (as Creighton points out) it
became a definite papal policy to side-track this pressure
for ecclesiastical reform into the direction of culture ;
popes staved off the Reformation by supporting the
Renaissance.   Men might be as pagan as they chose, so
long as they made no claim to be Bible-Christians, or
radical reformers in morals, or rivals to the temporal
sovereignty of the popes.   For that temporal sovereignty
was now a more practical reality than it had ever been
before ; now, at last, the popes were real and firmly-
seated princes of the City of Rome ; and they set themselves deliberately to dazzle their subjects, far and near,
by the most princely displays of earthly splendour.
Their palaces, and the new church of St. Peter's which
was now to replace the ancient building, ranked among
the marvels of the world.   To raise funds for St. Peter's,
indulgences were multiplied tenfold, though so devoted
a papalist as the Oxford Chancellor Gascoigne had already
complained of the system as intolerable.   It was these
Petrine indulgences, as everybody knows, which first
brought Luther forward.   The policy of side-tracking
had failed ; there were now two breaches in the ecclesiastical dyke, Reformation and Renaissance ; for indeed
that encouragement of culture soon proved, from the
narrowly ecclesiastical point of view, a short-sighted
policy.   Modern Catholic historians on the Continent,
who are generally far better-read and abler in every way

than their English brethren, recognize clearly that the worst enemy of orthodoxy has been not the Reformation but the Renaissance. It is not Protestantism which has gradually converted France into a country more anti-clerical than Great Britain, or which has prompted (if we are to believe the Catholic newspapers) far worse cruelties in modern Mexico than in Tudor England.

The more we insist upon the connexion of medieval art and religion, the more we must recognize how fatal this long sapping movement must have proved to Gothic art. That connexion, even when all exaggerations have been stripped away, was admittedly very strong. If it weakened visibly from the mid-thirteenth century onward, this was partly because rationalistic opposition to the Church was rapidly increasing at that same time. In any case, therefore, the Renaissance was likely to undermine Gothic art in something like the proportion in which it undermined orthodoxy ; but, as the movement gained momentum, and especially when popes and princes gave it their whole-hearted support on the artistic side, then social and economic forces came into play also ; and from thenceforward its victory was assured and irresistible.

Having thus noted the indirect action upon art through religion, let us go back to trace the more direct effects of this movement.

Here, again, the earlier manifestations are too often ignored. Father Cahier finds traces of Renaissance debasement in the France of the later fourteenth century.[1] He writes : " The confident expansion of this new art [more realistic than that of the thirteenth century] had its dangerous rock, as all human things have. By carrying men out of themselves, it tempted them to find pleasure in outward show rather than in inward principle. This inconvenience could only have been avoided if faith had kept her full sovereignty, or even increased it, in order to hallow these [purely] human

[1] *Nouveaux Mélanges*, 1877, pp. 187 ff.

accessories. That, unfortunately, was not the case. The outer world, at this time, grew abruptly and suddenly in action and in influence, while there were neglected, but powerful causes which sapped men's hearts and minds. . . . The desertion of several Christian populations was being prepared by turbulence and immorality ; and, when art was in full flower, towards the end of the fifteenth century, its sap was already running dry."

What is here said of France might be said more emphatically of Italy. Perrens brings out clearly the first stages of Renaissance art in Florence.[1] After instancing Giotto and his disciples, and quoting examples from 1360 to 1374, he continues : " If the nude was ill seen under ample draperies, the magnificence of the costumes, and the glorious feasts of a city where everyone lived in the open air, in the sun, under a blue sky, were food for art. And the nude was not quite absent, as may be thought. In Rome, and probably elsewhere, there were races of naked men as in the old games of Greece, and obscene processions as in the circuses of the Roman Empire, while the loose morals of the artists hardly induce a belief that they lacked occasions to study the nude. A change was promised not so much in art as in the condition of the artists. In old Florence an architect, a sculptor, or a painter was a tradesman like any other, and not distinguished from a mechanic ; for example, a varnisher was classed with a painter. . . . Under the oligarchy, in the relative calm that came with oppression, a taste for art as well as for letters began to develop in Florence as elsewhere." The study of the antique flourished ; and " by it Christian art was relegated to a second place. Building was continued, and churches were decorated, and it is a mistake to imagine that the Medici wanted to turn their compatriots from a religion that teaches submission to the great ; but there were churches everywhere ; what was wanted were palaces,

[1] *Hist. of Florence, from the Domination of the Medici*, tr. Lynch, 1892, vol. i, pp. 200 ff.

and in palaces pious pictures being out of place, hunting-scenes, tournaments, amorous and mythological adventures, served to recall ancient art, now so long forgotten as to appear quite fresh. . . . That Brunelleschi had lost what a few may call the sentiment of religion, which is only the tradition of the hieratic art of ancient times, we need not doubt. He built churches and palaces upon the same antique models. . . . But, like Giotto, he had the taste for natural forms. . . . He advanced art in the direction of truth and reality, and, in building temples for churches, incurred, like many others, the reproach of being a pagan. Not an unjustifiable reproach, certainly, but those who flung it at the fifteenth century ought to have included the fourteenth also. Piety and chastity were then not more frequent ; and, if the sentiment of religion was less rare, religion itself was wanting in purity. The Scaligeri of Verona, the Estes of Ferrara, the Della Polentas of Ravenna, the Malatestas of Rimini, the Visconti of Milan, Castruccio, Robert of Naples, and also [Pope] Clement V in his *lupanar* at Avignon, equalled the Medici in their appreciation of the famous mythological nudities which are said to have ruined Christian art. The only difference was that in the fourteenth century commissions for this sort of work were few, as it was not yet the fashion. If Giotto, of joyous and pagan temperament, only painted sacred and serious subjects, it was because he did not solely paint for pleasure, but also for bread. The strong impulsion of the Renaissance was necessary to force artists to free themselves from the prevailing taste by disinterested study, and little by little to transform it." Benozzo Gozzoli was a sceptic, ready to work either in the religious or the profane style ; Perugino's religious scepticism was notorious and impenitent. Lippo Lippi was the most profligate of all in his private life, but " his subjects were always religious . . . because his cloistered life procured him countless commissions . . . a proof that the paganism of the Renaissance did not exclude a taste for religious pictures."

Savonarola succeeded momentarily in stemming the more open paganisms and obscenities, and in converting a few painters, "but faith did not bring them back to the Christian traditions of art " ; " no sign of Christian faith is to be seen in the remarkable works of Simone del Pollaiuolo (1457–1508)." It was still fashionable to pay for sacred subjects, and profitable to paint them, but the great thirteenth-century tradition of art was already dead. New social ideas, and new economic forces, were sweeping it away.

New social ideas ; for the Middle Ages had their own natural thirst for novelty and change. I cannot help believing that the generality of men were no more artistic then than they are now ;[1] and that, if they did not show the frequent modern preference for thoroughly bad art, it was because there was no thoroughly bad art for them to choose. The apprenticeship and gild system, which hindered the highest flights of all, rendered impossible the vilest lapses ; those baser things against which Morris fought were never to be bought in the medieval market. But, if they had been, many men would have preferred them, just as thousands of purchasers in India prefer crude Manchester stuff to their own traditional native prints, not only because it is cheaper, but also because it is newer and more glaring.[1] So, in the Middle Ages, novelty attracted more than abstract beauty. Men tired of the noble architecture of the thirteenth century, and invented what we call the Decorated style ; they tired of that spiritual grace which is the main claim of Gothic statuary in comparison with that of antiquity ; they went on therefore, stage by stage, to complete realism. Then, again, the newer Perpendicular style (or, in France, the Flamboyant) gained a victory rather of fashion than of excellence ; and finally the Classical styles, new again after a sleep of a thousand years, began

[1] I must warn the reader that Professor Lethaby is unable to accept the opinions hazarded in these two sentences ; but they express my belief, and therefore I leave them for what they are worth.

to drive out all the rest. Eugène Müntz counts it as a very remarkable testimony to the originality and penetration of the future Pope Pius II that, in spite of his contempt for " the pictures of 200 years ago," he has real admiration for Giotto as the harbinger of a new school which " has now reached the summit of art," in other words, of the Renaissance school.[1] About this same time, " under Nicholas V [1447–55], glass-painting gave a last flicker before its systematic exclusion from Italian churches ; or, at least, before it ceased as an independent art, and became the handmaid of painting proper, and was reduced to the meanest of rôles, that of mere copyist."[2]

Thus, in the story of the Renaissance, we find the plainest corrective to all exaggerated identifications of Gothic art with any religious denomination, to the exclusion of others. Such exaggerations break down at once when we note how differently dogma and art reacted to this new current which attained its full strength in the early sixteenth century. Theologically, the Renaissance was a solvent of Roman Catholic tradition ; but, artistically, it was welcomed as the logical consequence of that tradition. The fact that medieval Church ceremonies were borrowed from pagan Rome is (argues de Gourmont), " the best proof of the antiquity and also of the excellence of Catholicism. . . . The most ancient religions are the best ; it is a great absurdity to try reducing children's games to reason ; it is great madness to attempt the purification of religions." And again : " A young Catholic poet has called the Blessed Virgin ' cette belle nymphe ' ; there is the true tradition of popular Catholicism " : " Leo X and Julius II could truly boast the name of *Pontifex Maximus* ; they were truly successors not only to St. Peter but also to the High Priest of Jupiter Capitolinus."[3] Therefore, under

[1] *Les arts à la cour des Papes*, 1878, p. 222. The whole passage is most significant for the Renaissance estimate of medieval letters and art.

[2] Ibid., p. 76.

[3] *La Culture des Idées*, pp. 137, 138, 174.

these Renaissance popes, it is natural to find pagan art gaining ground in the churches of Italy. Rimini is here a classical example ; again, " at a time when Bembo, a pope's secretary and a future cardinal, spoke of ' the hero Jesus Christ ' and ' the virgin goddess,' we need not be surprised that Philaretus sculptured the loves of Jupiter and Leda upon the very gates of the Vatican.[1] But we may find the same movement even north of the Alps. This is brought out by Didron in two essays of his *Annales archéologiques*. In the first (xii, 300) he discourses on " paganism in Christian art " ; in the second (xiii, 242) he describes and figures a painting of the Virgin Mary as Venus. It is an Assumption in a triptych of perhaps shortly before or after 1500, which he ascribes to a pupil of the Van Eycks or of Memling, and even guesses at the possibility of ascription to one of those masters himself. The engraving fully bears out his description : " The Mother of God is painted standing, absolutely naked, her dishevelled hair falling round her with the intention of supplying a garment which they certainly do not supply." And he adds in a footnote : " This Venus-Virgin was originally even less veiled than she is at present."

---

[1] Perrens, *l.c.*, p. 465.

CHAPTER XXII

RENAISSANCE AND DESTRUCTION

THE foregoing chapter has shown how naturally the revived pagan art began to supplant that of the Middle Ages ; let us turn now to the subject of deliberate destruction. The demolition of ancient work had been common enough in the Middle Ages ; but now at last, for the pleasure of popes and princes, it became chronic and systematic.

That famous White Robe of Churches, that sudden rush of new buildings, which marked the Cluniac revival, had involved considerable destruction of older edifices. In the words of the Cluniac Ralph Glaber, who is our authority for the whole episode, " the fabrics of churches were rebuilt, though many of these were still seemly and needed no such care ; but every nation in Christendom rivalled with the other, as to which should worship in the seemliest buildings." So again with the great outburst of architecture about A.D. 1200 ; so, again, when the Perpendicular style invaded England. The Totnes visitation of 1342 not infrequently insists that a church should be rebuilt because it is " small and dark " ; in other words, Norman or simple Early English. This was one side of the vigorous vitality of medieval art ; the weakest must go to the wall, and that weakest was nearly always the most ancient. In English churches, especially of the Perpendicular period, we commonly find fragments of Norman doorways or arcades built in with the ordinary rubble. A large number of early tombstones have been thus utilized for the walls of Bracebridge Church, near Lincoln, and of Little Shelford in Cambridgeshire. One fine medieval tombstone is

built into the tower staircase of Castleacre in Norfolk;
another, at Little Malvern, has been built into the
roof of an opening at the east end, where it can only
be detected by a person adventurous enough to clamber
into this niche. We have more records of vandalism
in tombs, perhaps, than in any other feature; in this
matter, we cannot distinguish between one medieval
century and another. At Troyes Cathedral, in 1385,
a new choir-screen was built and the old (which
to us would probably have seemed the nobler) was pulled
down. " The work employed fifteen men per diem. In
this clearing process they met with six tombs, four of
them to known persons, but they were unable to identify
two of the skeletons, though certain indications showed
that one was a bishop and the other a monk. The chapter,
without troubling farther about these illustrious dead,
caused them to be buried in plain coffins at threepence
apiece," the masons receiving fivepence a day.[1] When
Queen Philippa was buried in Westminster Abbey,
wrought iron rails were employed from the tomb of Bishop
Braybroke in St. Paul's Cathedral, to grace the queen's
sepulchre. Part of Philippa's own tomb, not long after,
was disfigured by building that of Henry V up against it.[2]
Henry V's queen, Katharine, had her own tomb cast
out from the Lady Chapel in 1502 : " Her coffin was to
lie unburied for more than two centuries and a half."[3]
A whole batch of seven early thirteenth century tombs
at Wells, and another batch of ten Perpendicular tombs
at Hereford, commemorate earlier bishops some of whom
perhaps never had monuments, but others had probably
been destroyed. The famous Johann Busch tells us
himself of what he did at Sulte, near Hildesheim. " Bishop
Brunyng, of Hildesheim, founded [the Abbey Church of
Sulte] . . . and lieth buried there by the choir door, in
a raised tomb which beareth the image of a bishop with

[1] Quicherat, *Mélanges*, vol. ii, p. 211.
[2] Lethaby, *Westminster I*, p. 251.
[3] Westlake, *Last Days*, p. 101.

mitre and crozier. When we reformed the monastery, we took that image away and put it in front of the principal altar . . . calling it that of St. Godhard [who had first founded the Church of Sulte before the monastery was founded], because my Lord Brunyng, though he had been a holy man, was not canonized. And we levelled Bishop Brunyng's tomb with the ground." This was about 1420.[1]   The monk Odo of St. Maur, writing in 1058, describes the beauty of Count Burchard's tomb, erected in the abbey church some forty years before. It bore, he says, " on his breast a gilded cross with the letters *alpha* and *omega* ; I also, in my boyhood, saw this with mine own eyes ; but all this has been utterly destroyed since, as we may see to-day." [2]   Richard of Barking, abbot of Westminster, was buried in the Lady Chapel " beneath a tomb of marble, which was destroyed in the time of Abbot Colchester." [3]   William of Malmesbury tells us that the tomb of the famous Joannes Scotus Eriugena had been destroyed before the date at which he was writing : this was done by Abbot Warin (1070–1081), who at the same time cast out the tombs of St. Maidulf and other great abbots of the past.[4]   Abbot Curteys of St. Edmundsbury, between 1436 and 1441, was compelled to fulminate against " the improper removals of sepulchral monuments from the cemetery of the [abbey] church." [5]   Some of the latest medieval work at Melrose Abbey destroyed, wholly or in part, large numbers of ancient tombs ; the walls " appear to have been founded on, or at least partially to cover, the tombstones of a previous generation. . . . Under it [the east wall] we find numbers of sepulchral stones showing black-letter inscriptions, and portions of incised figures, apparently crosses, etc., peeping out

[1] *Lib. Ref.*, bk. i, c. vi, p. 409.
[2] Migne, P. L., vol. clxiii, col. 860.
[3] Dugdale-Caley, vol. i, p. 271.
[4] R. L. Poole, *Ill. Hist. Med. Thought*, 2nd ed., 1920, p. 282.
[5] Dugdale-Caley, vol. iii, p. 114.

below the base of the wall."[1]   But perhaps the worst
record comes from St. Albans, where there were two
wholesale raids. Paul, the first Norman abbot (1077–93),
did " what can in no way be excused ; he destroyed the
tombs of his venerable predecessors the noble abbots,
whom he was wont to call rude and unlearned, either
despising them as English, or in envy, since almost all
had been born of royal stock, or the noble blood of great
lords." [2] Abbot Robert, again (1151–66), " in the first
construction of the chapter-house which he was about
to build, caused the bodies of the old abbots to be buried
too meanly [abjecte] and without counsel of discreet men,
at the counsel of his mason ; wherefore, when the mason
was cut off by apoplexy, the memory of the place was
lost." [3]

What was done with tombs was done in every other
quarter. St. Albans had a remarkable school of painters
in the early thirteenth century ; the remaining fragments
are now guarded with pious care, and inspire critics to
almost lyrical rhapsodies : " I can scarcely conceive of
anything finer than this series of paintings as viewed
from the west end of the church." Yet " those paintings
were probably all whitewashed over at the end of the
fourteenth or early in the fifteenth century, as it may
be noticed that a fifteenth century bracket, which we
know held the figure of St. Richard in 1428, has been
inserted into the middle of the lower picture of the first
painting." [4] For neither the ecclesiastical guardian of a
church, nor the artist who worked upon it, felt anything
like the modern conservatism. The saintly and learned
Odo Rigaldi, Archbishop of Rouen from 1248 to 1267,
more than once entered in his register a command that
church windows, not yet glazed, should be walled up for
convenience of the worshippers. Artists, again, were

---

[1] Proc. Soc. Ant. Scotland, vol. ii, 1858, p. 174.
[2] Gest. Abb. S. Albani, R.S., vol. i, p. 62.
[3] Ibid., p. 183.
[4] Archæologia, vol. lviii, pp. 281–2.

naturally far more concerned to show their own powers and to go their own way than simply to patch up their predecessor's work, or to continue it with the fidelity of a pupil carrying out a master's designs. The magnificent thirteenth-century wheel window at Lynn, resembling but surpassing those in the west front of Peterborough Cathedral, had apparently become ruinous by about 1450. Instead of renewing it, the mason inserted a Perpendicular design more curious than beautiful, and used the old work to mend the roof of a turret staircase, where it was only discovered at the restoration of 1870. Very few people, in 1450, would have admitted Ruskin's Lamp of Memory : " Let us think, as we lay stone on stone, that a time will come when those stones will be held sacred because our hands have touched them. . . . The greatest glory of a building is not in its stones, nor in its gold. Its glory is in its age. . . . I think that a building cannot be considered as in its prime until four or five centuries have passed over it, and that the entire choice and arrangement of its details should have reference to their appearance after that period."[1] The medieval view was far more childlike than this. Those who looked forward at all were convinced that the world had not many years more to last ; few medieval expressions are more constant and uniform than this, that the world was at its last stage, deserving dissolution and destined soon to be dissolved. Men's childlike exuberance of invention was matched by childlike impatience and love of novelty : " There is more respect and consideration shown at the present moment to our cathedrals than was ever paid them in the Middle Ages."[2]

Our modern churchwardens have had their reasons for loving whitewash, but their forefathers had reason also. Constantly, in building accounts, we find a final entry : " *item*, for so many loads of lime," to wash the building over. It was not only that limewash is one of the most

---

[1] *Seven Lamps*, VI, x (p. 339 of the pocket authorized edition).
[2] *York Fabric Rolls*, p. 68, note.

PERPENDICULAR SUBSTITUTE FOR THE
LYNN WHEEL-WINDOW.

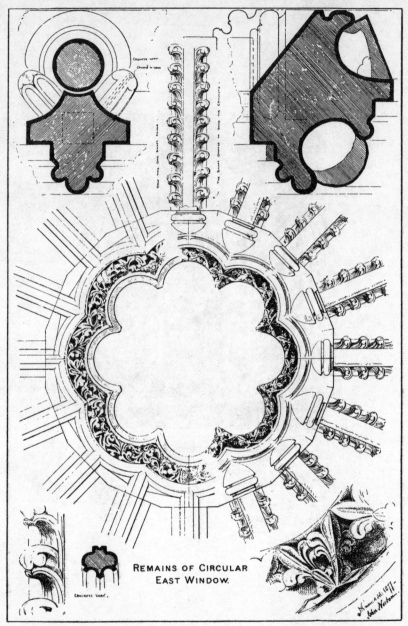

CRVCKETS VARY
CLYED IN SOME

OVER HERE ONE SHAFT FROM

THE SHAFT CENTRE IS WITH THE CRVCKETS

REMAINS OF CIRCULAR
EAST WINDOW.

CRVCKETS VARY.

John Norton

THIRTEENTH-CENTURY WINDOW FROM ST. MARGARET'S, LYNN.

valuable preservatives of stonework, but men loved it for itself ; it made their work look fresh and new. The White Tower, one of the glories of London, was thus distinguished and kept in constant brilliancy by royal command. The *Liberate Rolls* of 25 Hen. III contain a prescription to the Keeper of the Tower " to cause all the leaden gutters of the great towers through which rain water should fall from the summit of the same tower, to be carried to the ground ; so that the walls of the said tower, which has been newly whitewashed, may in no wise be injured by the dropping of rain water, nor be easily weakened." And in 1380, at Troyes, where the north transept, though only sixty years old, was already tarnished by weather, the cathedral chapter caused the whole gable and the rose window, with other portions, to be whitewashed.[1]

Moreover, it must be recognized that the childish love of destruction for destruction's sake was present also in the Middle Ages. Not only were many churches destroyed then, as now, for military reasons in war-time ; the thing was often done also, for military reasons or otherwise, in times of peace. The Emperor Charles V, champion of orthodoxy, ready to burn an unlimited number of heretics, deliberately swept away the church and nearly all the other buildings of one of the most beautiful abbeys in Europe, St. Bavon-de-Gand, in order to build a fortress which should overawe the too democratic citizens of Ghent.[2] Rufus's wholesale destruc-tion of churches for the sake of his own hunting in the New Forest may be ascribed partly to the irreligion of a monarch who, though he feared the Holy Face of Lucca, had little respect for any other religious idea, even as religious ideas were commonly conceived in his own time. But the Cistercian monks destroyed many churches

[1] Quicherat, *Mélanges, II*, 203.

[2] The whole story in V. Fris, *Hist. de Gand*, Brussels, 1913, pp. 192–3. I give a bird's-eye view of the abbey, taken just before its destruction, in the 2nd volume of *Five Centuries of Religion*.

in the thirteenth century, and so did sheep-farming abbots in the early sixteenth.[1] Then, in war-time (which, after all, was almost chronic in some of what are now among the most prosperous districts in Europe), very much was destroyed out of pure wantonness, as by Cromwell's troopers in later days. Father Denifle's two bulky volumes, *La désolation des Églises*, etc., give abundant evidence of this for the single country of France after the Hundred Years' War ; more harm was often done by the French royal troops, the francs-archers, to their own churches, than by the English invaders. More than one collection of miracles, again, testifies to the wanton vandalism of soldiers or desperate gamblers, and records the vengeance taken by saints whose images had been outraged. The chronicler Bourdigné, for instance, writing in 1521, tells us how " in the village called St.-Côme-de-Ver, in the said country of Maine, as the francs-archers aforesaid had (according to their wont) done several insolences and derisions against the holy relics in that church, and against the sacraments and ceremonies of the Church, finally one of them came behind the said church of St.-Côme, hard by the [great] glass window which giveth it light, where the said franc-archer found an apple-tree laden with fruit, which apples he plucked one by one, and threw them for his pleasure against the painted window of the church. And, having thrown several without being able to strike or break the glass, then it befel that, cursing and blaspheming, he cast one wherewith he smote the crown on a pictured St. Cosmas that was in the window ; which apple stuck there amidst the glass for a whole year's space, in the sight of all people, without decay or corruption ; yet on the other hand all the other apples that hung on the tree fell to the ground from that day forward, and rotted in the twinkling of an eye, as though poisoned and infected by the touch of that wretch who had laid hands on the tree ; who nevertheless escaped

[1] Documentary evidence for this may be found in my *Medieval Village*.

not our Lord's judgment and vengeance. For, in that night following, the arm wherewith he had cast the said apples was stricken with palsy."[1] And, finally, there was the vandalism of the general public. The friar Salimbene of Parma tells us of an old noble whom he had known in his boyhood, somewhere about A.D. 1230. " He came and dwelt hard by the Cathedral Church, which is dedicated to the glorious Virgin, wherein he daily heard Mass and all the daily and nightly offices of the Church, each at the fit season ; and, whensoever he was not busied with the offices of the Church, he would sit with his neighbours under the public portico by the Bishop's palace, and speak of God, or listen gladly to any who spoke of Him. Nor would he ever suffer children to cast stones against the Baptistery or the Cathedral to destroy the carvings or paintings ; for when he saw any such he waxed wroth and ran swiftly against them and beat them with a leather thong as though he had been specially deputed to this office ; yet he did it for pure godly zeal and divine love, as though he said in the Prophet's words ' The zeal of thine house hath eaten me up.' " Again, the diary of the Florentine apothecary Landucci gives us, no less casually, just the same sort of evidence. When Michael Angelo had completed his colossal statue of David, and it was being slowly moved from his studio to its place in the public square, precautions were taken against the vandalism of the Florentine populace : " During the night, stones were thrown at the giant to injure it ; therefore it was necessary to keep watch over it." [2]

All this destruction was now immensely hastened by that economic development which was one important factor in both Renaissance and Reformation. Bishop

[1] *Chroniques*, vol. ii, p. 329, translated in *Medieval Garner*, 1st ed., p. 721.

[2] Landucci, p. 214 (May 14, 1504).

Creighton put it with his usual epigrammatic clearness :
"[In the fifteenth century] it was not because there
was a multitude of eager and able architects that churches
were built ; but because a number of wealthy wool
merchants wished to commemorate their munificence,
and had no better way of doing it than in pulling down
the old parish church and building another. We see
what the fifteenth century built, not what it destroyed.
Yet we admire as rare gems the fine Norman, Early
English, and Decorated churches, on a smaller scale,
which still remain in the lucky villages which did not
produce a wealthy man, who ground down the people
during his life and then built a new church to serve as
a chantry to himself." [1]   In short, the wool-merchant was
now doing on a smaller scale what popes and princes
were doing in papal and princely proportions. Nowhere,
perhaps, in any civilized community, has there been such
wholesale and persistent vandalism as in the City of
Rome. Here, if anywhere, the modern artist may
moralize sadly on that which man hath made of man.
The story is told briefly by the Jesuit professor Grisar
in his *History of Rome and the Popes in the Middle Ages*,
and by the still more learned Lanciani in his *Destruction
of Ancient Rome* (Macmillans, 1899). And it is so vital
to the whole thesis of this present book, that I give it
as far as possible in Lanciani's own words.

From the moment when this city began to revive from
the torpor of the Dark Ages, and the times of worst
ignorance and immorality among the popes, it began also
systematically to pursue the revival of its own art through
the destruction of Græco-Roman work. Rome became
famous for delicate work in the purest white marble,
inlaid with mosaics of the most costly materials ; and it
was one of these Roman workmen, Peter, whom Henry III
employed for the magnificent shrine which he erected
in honour of Edward the Confessor in Westminster
Abbey. This work, exported thus to far-off England (or,

[1] *Life and Letters*, ed. Louise Creighton, vol. i, p. 413.

to give another instance, to Aachen), has generally been called *Cosmati*, after the most famous family which earned a living by it.   But in fact it demanded the energies of several families, which seem to have formed a sort of close corporation.   We find the " filii Pauli " in about 1150, the " filii Cosmati " about 1180, " Vassalecti " from 1153 to 1275, and a fourth branch from 1143 to 1209 : " For three centuries this guild lived and prospered and accomplished its work at the expense of the ruins of ancient Rome."[1]   For the bulk of this work, the pure white foundation was obtained by cutting up Greek statues of Parian marble ; and the other precious materials were broken from porphyry columns, ancient mosaics, and every place where rare Eastern stones could be found.   The first influential voice heard in remonstrance against these practices of the marble-cutters, and the utter abandonment of the Roman monuments, is that of Petrarch.   But the great poet pleaded in vain ; for the destruction did not decrease in the Middle Ages and it waxed even greater in the Renaissance.   Chrysoloras, the master of Poggio Bracciolini, says, referring to marbles taken from this source : " The statues lie broken in fragments, ready for the lime-kiln, or are made use of as building material. I have seen many used as mounting steps, or as curbstones, or as mangers in stables."   In 1426, the papal authorities gave a company of lime-burners leave to destroy the Basilica Julia, claiming half the produce of the kilns ; a host of other monuments were thus destroyed. " ' In the early years of Paul III ' (1534–1550), says De Marchi, ' many torsoes and statues discovered in digging cellars, in planting gardens and vineyards, and in opening new streets, used to be thrown into the kilns, especially those sculptured in Greek marble, on account of the wonderful lime which they produced. Paul III issued most cruel regulations to the effect that no one should dare thus to destroy ancient statuary

[1] Lanciani, p. 181 ; my other quotations come from succeeding pages of the same book.

under penalty of death.' As a matter of fact, however, these 'most cruel regulations' of Paul III did not produce a lasting effect. We may suppose that the destruction of the masterpieces of Græco-Roman art may have diminished for the time being, but it was by no means suppressed. The spoliation of marble and stone edifices went on with increasing activity to the end of the sixteenth century. We must not forget that another edict of the same pope, dated July 22, 1540, put at the mercy of the 'deputies' of the Fabbrica di S. Pietro [i.e. St. Peter's Church at Rome] all the monuments of the Forum and of the Sacra Via ; and they did not hesitate to profit by the pontifical grant to the fullest possible extent. Pirro Ligorio, the architect, discussing the best way of obtaining a particularly fine plaster, suggests the use of powdered Parian marble, 'obtained from the statues which are constantly destroyed.' . . . Fra Giocondo da Verona, adducing testimony from his own experience, says that some Roman citizens boasted of having had the foundations of their houses and palaces constructed with ancient statues. . . . So important was the exercise of this industry of lime-burning at the Circus Flaminius that the whole district received the name of Lime-pit (calcarario, calcararia). . . . In fact, none of the important excavations with which I have been connected, either in Rome or on neighbouring sites, has failed to bring to light remains of one or more lime-kilns. I mention two examples as specially worthy of note. A lime-kiln was found in the palace of Tiberius on the Palatine hill by Rosa, in 1869. It was filled to the brim with fine works of art, some calcined, some intact. Among the latter were the veiled bust of Claudius, now in the Museo delle Terme ; a head of Nero ; three caryatides, in nero antico ; the exquisite little statuette of an ephebus in black basalt, published by Hauser in the *Mittheilungen* for 1895, pp. 97–119, pl. 1 ; a head of Harpocrates, and other minor fragments. In February 1883, in the excavations on the south side of the Atrium of Vesta, a pile of marble was found about 14 feet long, 9 feet wide and 7 feet high. It was wholly made up of statues of the *Vestales maximæ*, some unbroken, others in fragments. The statues and fragments had been carefully packed together, leaving as few interstices as possible between them, and the spaces formed by the curves of the bodies were filled in with chips. . . . These beautiful statues had been piled into a regular oblong, like a cord of wood, by some diggers of marble, who had carefully filled the spaces between the statues as they lay side by side, in order that no empty spaces might be left. By what fortunate accident these sculptures were preserved it is difficult to guess ; but one thing at least is certain—a great quantity of other marbles belonging to the House of the Vestals must have perished by fire. Two kilns and two deposits of lime and of charcoal were found in the course of the same excavations." Lanciani gives a list of specially papal demolitions (p. 201). " Alexander VI destroyed also a Forum, a temple, and part of the Baths of Diocletian. His successor, Julius II " (1503–1513), had too many wars in hand to afford much time or money for destroying ancient monuments ; but he laid the foundations of the present St. Peter's, and destroyed the old church.[1] " The loss occasioned to art, history, and Christian antiquities by the destruction of the venerable basilica is simply incalculable. The west half of the greatest temple of Christendom was levelled to the ground with all its precious decorations in mosaic, fresco, sculpture, in marble and in wood, with its historical inscriptions and its pontifical tombs, among which were those of Celestine IV († 1243), Gregory IX († 1241), Boniface IX († 1404), Innocent VII († 1406), Eugene IV († 1447) and Nicholas V (†1455). Three other churches also disappeared in the pontificate of Julius II. . . . No great losses are recorded under the rule of Leo X. . . . The only act of vandalism which can be brought home to him is the destruction of a certain part of the Via

[1] The destruction had been begun by Nicholas V (Müntz, 1878, p. 105).

Tiburtina, called La Quadrata, the embankment of which was supported by great walls of travertine. The stones were removed to St. Peter's." After which he sums up (p. 202) : " All sense of the beautiful, all appreciation of art, seems to have been lost for a time among the Romans. While other cities in Italy were raising churches, town-halls, exchanges, fountains, palaces, and splendid private houses which command admiration at the present day on account of the graceful simplicity of their proportions and the finish of their work, the builders at Rome did little more than pile up and jumble together fragments of older structures without regard to form or fitness. Tivoli, Viterbo, and even Corneto, were in this period far superior to Rome in their public and domestic architecture. They can point to splendid examples of the skill and taste of their master masons of the fourteenth century, while we Romans have absolutely nothing to show that is comparable."[1]

In another volume, Lanciani emphasizes the full responsibility of the Renaissance for vandalism.

" In the long and sad history of the destruction of ancient Rome, the Middle Ages are perhaps the least guilty—less guilty, at any rate, than the period of the Renaissance which followed. In spite of their enthusiastic love for ancient art and classic civilization, the great masters of the Renaissance treated our monuments and ruins with incredible contempt and brutality. The original cause of this state of things must be found, strange to say, in the increasing civilization of the age, in the softening and refining of former habits, in the development of public and private wealth, which was pushing popes, cardinals, patricians, bankers, and rich merchants to raise everywhere magnificent palaces and villas, churches and monasteries, aqueducts and fountains, harbours and bridges, castles and towers. All these constructions of the golden age, which justly form the pride

[1] *Ancient Rome*, Macmillans, 1888. My quotations come from the preface, xvi ff.

of my city, and make it unique and enviable by the whole world, were built, stone by stone, with materials stolen from ancient ruins. . . . The cinquecento excavations did more harm to the monuments of imperial, republican, and kingly Rome than the ten centuries of preceding barbarism. . . . The next period, which runs from the middle of the seventeenth century to the end of the eighteenth, ranks also among the saddest in our history, because it marks the almost complete destruction of medieval buildings. Under the pretence of restorations and embellishments, the authorities laid their hands upon the most noted and the most venerable churches of the city, which had until then preserved their beautiful basilical type in all its simplicity, purity and majesty."

He goes on to enumerate, from 1665 onwards, thirteen great churches thus spoiled; and he adds : " The system followed in restoring these churches was everywhere uniform. The columns of the nave were walled up, and concealed in thick pilasters of whitewashed masonry ; the inscribed or sculptured marble slabs and the mosaic pavements were taken up and replaced by brick floors ; the windows were enlarged out of all proportion, and assumed a rectangular form, so that floods of light might enter and illuminate every remote, peaceful recess of the sacred place. For the beautiful roofs made of cedar wood, vaults or *lacunaria* were substituted. The number of entrance-doors was trebled ; the simple but precious frescoes of the fourteenth century were whitewashed, and the fresh surface was covered with the insignificant productions of Francesco Cozza, Gerolamo Troppa, Giacinto Brandi, Michelangelo Cerruti, Pasquale Marini, Biagio Puccini, and other painters equally obscure. All these profanations could be accomplished, not only without opposition, but amid general applause, because such was the spirit of the age." It needed a special art-lover like Vasari to raise any protest against the demolition of medieval work. He laments the destruction of a very valuable fresco by Pietro Cavallini

in San Marco at Florence, which, with many other
similar works of art, was whitewashed over, " with little
feeling or consideration," by the Dominicans, the brethren
of Fra Angelico. In 1560, at S. Spirito in Florence, the
monks destroyed a priceless fresco by Simone Memmi.[1]
In fact, though there was perhaps more religious painting
done now than ever before, and though purely pagan
subjects were still only a minority, yet the prevailing
taste was strongly anti-medieval.

Again, there is perhaps no matter for which iconoclasts
have earned bitterer curses than for their destruction of
stained glass, one of the most precious heritages of
medieval art. Much of this, of course, was done deliberately for religious reasons ; but surely, if any excuse
can be admitted for this destruction, that is the best
that could be pleaded. When popes themselves decreed
the destruction of certain representations, without for
one moment taking their artistic merits into consideration, must not the average thinking man of to-day recognize some palliation for a similar destruction of imagery
which proclaimed doctrines inextricably intermingled,
at that time, with superstitions and cruelties which no
man dares to defend at the present day. The worship of
the Virgin Mary, the doctrine of Transubstantiation,
were things for which hundreds had suffered the cruellest
of deaths, and for which other thousands or even millions
were still liable, under Roman Catholic law, to be burned
at any time. This system was deliberately described, by
incomparably the greatest Roman Catholic historian who
ever wrote in the English language, in terms which will
be questioned by few scholars who have actually studied
the Inquisition records, and searched their own hearts
unsparingly as to the real meaning of those documents.

[1] *Lives of the Painters*, Bohn, vol. i, pp. 179, 184. Yet Cavallini had
enjoyed such a reputation for personal piety in his own day that, as
Vasari says, it is no wonder a crucifix made by him actually spoke to St.
Bridget, and that a Virgin of his " should have performed, and still be
performing, an infinite number of miracles." For farther instances of
vandalism see Schlosser, *Beiträge*, pp. 93, 123, 143.

" The principle of the Inquisition," wrote Acton, " is murderous " ; and, again : " The murder of a heretic was not only permitted but rewarded . . . it was a virtuous deed to slaughter Protestant men and women, until they were all exterminated."[1]   In the face of a system which can be thus described by a man of ency-clopædic learning and supremely conscious of the his-torian's responsibilities, which of us will refuse some measure of sympathy, at least, to men who believed that the highest of all arts is the conduct of life ; and that, if even the most marvellous picture is murderous of soul and body, then the world will gain by its disappearance ? This, after all, is what inspired Savonarola, though of course his definition of soul-murder would have differed widely in many ways from that of the Reformers. A century earlier, the same religious zeal in face of the relics of an earlier worship had inspired Urban V, one of the three best popes of the fourteenth century. " On the throne of St. Peter, he lived as a monk faithful to the smallest details of his Rule " ; he always confessed before saying his Mass ; " the impulse which he gave to art was no less strong than that which he gave to letters and to science " ; and he had the courage to bring the papal court from Avignon back to Rome, if only for a few months. But he fought hard against what he con-sidered immodesty in the fashionable dress of his day ; and, under the foundations of the vast palace which he was building, he deliberately buried a statue of Hercules and other objects of pagan art " in order to abolish the memory of idolatry."[2] St.-Francois de Sales, again, de-stroyed many medieval statues in his diocese as unedify-ing.[3] Would there not have been equal moral justification for any Protestant ruler who, if he had had the power, might have destroyed artistic representations which

[1] *Letters to Mary Gladstone*, 1904, pp. 141, 185.

[2] G. Mollat, *Papes d'Avignon*, 1st ed., pp. 105, 109 ; J. B. Joudou, *Hist. de la ville d'Avignon*, 1853, p. 393.

[3] *Rev. hist. franciscaine*, vol. iv, 1927, p. 207.

tended to assert the world-authority of the Pope ; that is, of another ruler who claimed over all baptized persons the power of life and death for differences of belief, and who frequently put that claim into practice ? Christ of the Bible, when Peter rushed into the crowd and cut off the ear of Malchus, reproved that action in words of unmistakable rebuke : " All that take the sword shall perish with the sword." Yet the Bible of the Poor, at Reims, tells us a very different story. The incident there is portrayed not according to the Gospels, but after the mystic gloss which represents it as an exercise of legitimate judicial authority ; not a disorderly affray, but as a solemn and deliberate execution. A passage wrongly attributed to St. Gregory the Great, but really from St. Ambrose, is incorporated in Gratian's *Decretum*, the first book of that *Corpus Juris Canonici* by which the Church, and to a great extent the State also, was regulated almost entirely for the last three and a half centuries of the Middle Ages. It is from a commentary upon Luke xxii, 50 and John xviii, 10, with which we must compare Matt. xxvi. 51, and it is headed : *The Roman Church, by her Profession of Faith, hath cut off the ear of Error.* In the text we find : " Peter, therefore, cutteth off the ear. But why Peter ? Because it is he who hath received the keys of the Kingdom of Heaven. For he doth condemn who doth also absolve, since he hath received the power both of binding and of loosing. So he smiteth off the ear of him who listeneth ill ; he smiteth off with the spiritual sword the inward ear of him who understandeth wrongly." And the commentary upon this runs : " Peter, at our Lord's passion, cut off the ear of Malchus, and the Lord restored it again ; note thereby that it is Peter's duty to cut off spiritually the ear of him who understandeth wrongly, for he hath the power of binding and loosing. Note also that, if such men be converted, God will restore their hearing."[1] This, then, is the doctrine which the Reims sculptor has

[1] Pars. ii, caus. xxiv, q.1, cap. 17.

PETER AND MALCHUS AT REIMS.

ST. JOHN'S COLLEGE LIBRARY.

represented in preference to the Bible story. Instead of the generous ill-regulated impulse of the disciple, plunging hastily into the crowd with a blow which was misdirected even more from the spiritual than from the military point of view, here we have a judge quietly and deliberately executing justice upon an offender paralysed by his sense of guilt. Malchus clings to the operating Peter with the same passive resignation with which, in our childhood, we clung to the dentist's chair. This distortion of Bible facts, however, was perfectly natural in the circumstances. By the time this group was carved, in the middle or the latter half of the thirteenth century, popes were asserting the right of wielding not only the spiritual but also the earthly sword, even against emperors and princes. Not only did they claim to make and unmake kings, and to transfer whole populations from one ruler to another, but they had more than once set armies in motion to enforce that claim. It is more than probable, therefore, that this was in the mind of the man who conceived the Reims group ; and it is practically certain that the sculpture would convey that impression to those who took the Reims portals for their Bible. Therefore, as we can say of the Doom, that it was not only a work of art but even more definitely a sermon, so these two Reims figures must be considered in that double aspect ; and any inartistic person who might care for nothing but the moral lesson would be more truly in the mind of the Church than a beholder of the most sensitive artistic fibre who remained indifferent to that lesson. But the moral in this case is, at bottom, political ; the group, in its inner meaning, begs a party-question no less important than that question of the flag which stands so definitely in the front rank, at the present moment, in South Africa and in Germany. If this relation of Peter to Malchus, of the Church to the State, could have been expounded to one of the earlier Christian emperors, or even to Charles the Great, it would have seemed as revolutionary to him as the Declaration of

Independence. Any earthly ruler, therefore, who might have demanded the defacement of that Reims group would simply have been paying the Church the compliment of taking her to mean what she said. " If, indeed, it stands there mainly to teach a lesson, then I cannot tolerate a lesson which seems to me so false." If that lesson had been expounded to the Huguenot-hating Louis XIV, these statues would probably have run more risk of destruction from him than even from Henry IV in his Huguenot days. And in that case would not the dispassionate outsider have judged that, in this lamentable affair, the original fault lay with those who had mixed up good art with bad or questionable politics ? Consequently, regrettable as most of the sixteenth-century vandalism was, yet a great deal of it could at least plead such religious reasons as appeal perhaps to the majority of Christians to-day, and moral reasons which appeal to all men who refuse to admit heresy-hunting as an integral part of the Christian's duty to God.

If, therefore, as lovers of art, we feel bound to curse any of our predecessors, let us reserve our heartiest maledictions for those who, having no objection to the doctrines—being, indeed, professionally bound to burn such fellow-Christians as might publicly object to these doctrines—yet destroyed acres (it might almost be said) of priceless glass, through pure artistic indifference or actual dislike of those most characteristic medieval glories. Here again, instead of making my own summary from the sight of existing French cathedrals and the study of the pertinent monographs, let me translate from Olivier Merson, who gives the whole story briefly in his monograph on stained glass.[1]

" Now, if so many monuments of our national art have been destroyed, we must not seek the causes of this merely

---

[1] *Les Vitraux*, Quantin, 1895, p. 100. Our English churches, in spite of all ravages, contain probably twice as much medieval stained glass as there is in all the churches of Italy ; and I am told that Spain is not much better in that respect.

in the savagery of the religious wars or in the effervescence
of revolutionary rage, nor again in the folly of the ' black
bands ' or in human negligence. The very men who
ought to have been interested in preserving the glass have
often decided, nay, even commanded, its destruction.
At Notre-Dame-de-Paris, the chapter replaced all the
windows of the twelfth, thirteenth, and fourteenth
century with white glass. The canons of Reims, between
1739 and 1768, wrought this same act of vandalism in
the lower windows of their cathedral. Similar work was
done by the monks of St.-Remi-de-Reims ; and a worthy
Benedictine (Dom Chastellain, in order that his name
be not ignored), a learned man, we may suppose, wrote
with ineffable serenity on this matter : ' In order to give
this great basilica an air of majesty and magnificence
which it hitherto lacked, the monks, not content with
having put nearly all the windows into white glass a few
years earlier, undertook now to whitewash the church
again from top to bottom, which lasted from October
1755 to October 1757, and made it look quite new.'
Similarly at Chartres, in 1757, the canons took it into
their heads to replace the borders of twelve clerestory
windows in the choir with white glass ; and later (in 1773
and 1788) they ordered the total demolition of six of
these windows in order to throw a better light upon a
marble group by the [contemporary] sculptor Bridan,
representing the Assumption. In 1786, when Bridan
was finishing his work on the spot, the chapter had already
destroyed a great window of stained glass above the
temporary choir installed in the nave, near the south
transept. How many misdeeds were committed by
ordinary parish priests, when their hierarchical superiors,
and the best educated among the clergy, showed such a
burning love for white glass and whitewash ! Yet, in
spite of all, many thirteenth century windows have
managed to escape from untoward circumstances."

Here, again, is Canon J. Fossey's account of the carved
reredoses, in wood or stone, over a considerable portion

of Normandy.[1]   He can enumerate sixteen survivors ;
but he adds : " How many charming compositions of
this kind were destroyed by the bad taste of the seventeenth and eighteenth centuries ! Scarcely any one of
these is in its original place. They have been banished
either to the nave-walls, or even into the sacristies."

The men who did all this were untouched by the
Reformation ; but the Renaissance had cleft an impas-
sable chasm between them and medieval art. Modern
French Gothic, both in building and in furniture, is
definitely inferior to English of the same date ; and
perhaps nowhere is this so marked as in glass, which the
monk Theophilus specified as the unique glory of France.[2]

---

[1] *L'art religieux dans les diocèses de Rouen et d'Évreux* (Évreux, 1920,
p. 94).

[2] Here, again, I must insert a protest from Professor Lethaby : " No,
superior, in not being so *sham*." Yet I cannot help thinking that, from
this point of view also, the comparison holds good ; the church of
Bonsecours above Rouen, and the west front of St.-Ouen, seem as reprehensible shams as equivalent buildings of the same date on our side.

CHAPTER XXIII

RENAISSANCE AND CONSTRUCTION.—(1)

LET us now turn from the negative to the positive aspect of the Renaissance. This chapter will be found to owe a heavy debt to a stimulating modern writer on economics, Werner Sombart. The main theory of his two monographs on *War and Capitalism, Luxury and Capitalism,* and of his greater *Modern Capitalism* seems as sound as it is striking; and here and there it is possible to reinforce his argument by earlier instances than he has adduced.[1]

The thesis of the two books may be put into a single sentence; modern capitalism was not produced so much by any popular demand or popular effort, as by the pressure of war and luxury; it has been rather imposed from above than grown up from below. Modern industry on a large scale (*Gross-Industrie*) is differentiated from earlier and simpler society, among other factors, by two of supreme importance: the Contract System and Standardization. Both of those factors are due mainly to war and to luxury.

In one sense, the monks are the parents of modern Gross-Industrie. It was they who continued, or revived, that wholesale exploitation of the land which great Roman capitalists had practised in their *latifundia*. It was they alone who had capital enough to build on a scale rivalling or surpassing kings and princes. This capital, for many generations, they used more wisely

---

[1] *Krieg und Kapitalismus,* Leipzig, 1913; *Luxus und Kapitalismus,* Leipzig, 1913; *Der Moderne Kapitalismus,* vol. ii, pt. ii (Munich and Leipzig, 1919). I shall refer to these as K.K. and L.K. and M.K. respectively.

than other folk. What the serf would never have done for himself, he did under compulsion for himself and for the monk his master. The peasant was too content with mere animal nourishment for himself and his family, and too much hampered by narrowness of outlook and petty jealousies, to have brought things forward at anything like the rate which they actually took. The real capitalists, until the rise of a powerful merchant class, were the Benedictines and other almost equally wealthy Religious.[1] Petrus Cantor of Notre-Dame-de-Paris, one of the most pious and learned of the later twelfth century theologians, emphasizes this strongly. The luxury of contemporary building seems to him positively unchristian. Great folk everywhere are raising palaces as proud as the Tower of Babel; monks castellate their dwellings, in order to obtain farther security for their great wealth. If Peter had been told that this movement which he describes, after growing steadily for three centuries more, would suddenly bring men farther in a couple of generations than in the whole of those three hundred years, then he would probably have looked upon the world as past redemption.

Yet this is what history shows us. The prince or great baron or monk of the thirteenth century was a strong man armed; but the last generations of the Middle Ages produced a stronger than he had been. We have already seen how, two centuries after Peter, the author of *Dives and Pauper* finds more worldliness than religion in the great buildings of his own day.[2] The kitchen of the great cathedral monastery at Durham, which is still standing as a remarkable architectural monument, cost a sum equivalent to something like £15,000 in modern purchasing power. That of Canterbury Cathedral cost about the same; and, though a good deal of the food cooked in both found its way, sooner or later, to the

[1] Fuller evidence in the opening chapters of *Five Centuries of Religion*, vol. ii.

[2] Com. I, chap. li.

poor, yet this was far less than is commonly represented, and great abbeys often sold, instead of giving away, their offal and even the bones from the kitchen. One of the mainsprings of the Franciscan movement was a revolt against Benedictine capitalism; yet one of the most imposing buildings in Italy was built over St. Francis's bones within a few years of his death; and, when the author of *Piers Plowman's Creed* wishes to draw a satirical contrast between ideal and practice, he chooses the magnificent edifices of the professionally-mendicant Dominicans.

The Monastic Orders, then, did much to hasten the growth of wholesale production on a great scale; and war provided an even greater stimulus. I know no author who has brought out the influence of warfare upon art so well as Prof. Baldwin Brown; it cannot be expressed better than he has expressed it in a single page: " Nor was war less prolific [than religion] in commissions to the artist. Imperiously practical, as it has just been called, war demanded of all its impedimenta active service and not show, but the conditions that made the medieval an artistic epoch so wrought here, that display became one of the most effective agents for the work in hand. It was not for mere show, but for added efficiency in the camp and in the mêlée, that the sun was made to glint on the warrior's surcoat of crimson silk and gold, on the ridge and hollow of the fluted mail, on the embossed leather and the Damascene filigree in the iron of the horse trappings. The helm which kept safe his head within its walls of steel marked at the same time with crest and plume his progress through the ranks, while the sword with which he hewed his way had won by service its right to the gold and gems and costly fancies of the craftsmen lavished on its hilt. A whole minute and sumptuous art, that of heraldry, was brought into being to exalt his personal distinction and pride of race, and he confronted the foe with the insignia of his person and line emblazoned on his shield; all the arts of the time vied with each other to give to his tomb a glory that should be record and praise in one."[1]

But we are dealing here with a special stimulus, the stimulus to Gross-Industrie. We have already seen, in Chapter XVII, how the citizens of Ardres were conscripted wholesale to fortify that town ; and there are many similar medieval records on a smaller scale. It may be safely asserted, I think, that in every city the compulsory levy for raising or repairing walls, whether in labour or in money, preceded by many generations, or even by many centuries, such a contribution as the paving-rate or any similar modern levy. Aigues-Mortes was evidently built by concentrating labour on a very great scale ; so was a princely castle like the now-vanished Coucy ; so, as we know from documentary evidence, was Windsor Castle. Most significant is a note quoted from the Close Rolls of 28 Henry III by Prof. Lethaby : " In 1244 the king ordered the same keepers to see that the Knight's Chamber in the Palace of Westminster should be finished before Easter, even if they had to employ a thousand men. This employment of a thousand men is a characteristic exaggeration in the king's speech, of which there are many examples. The Sheriff of Kent in 1244–5 was instructed to prevent stone being taken to London except for the works of Westminster. London was to suffer a great deal on account of these same works!"[2]

Of special interest, again, is the passage in Lydgate's *Troy Book* in which he describes Priam's royal haste to build that city ; a passage which enlarges upon the scene in far fuller detail than the original from which Lydgate borrows :

> " And all about the countries environ
> He madë seek in every region
> For suchë workmen as were curious,
> Of wit inventive, of casting marvellous,

---

[1] *Arts in Early England*, vol. i, p. 7.
[2] Lethaby I, p. 150.

Or such as couldë craft of ge[o]metry
Or werë subtle in their fantasy;
And for every that was good deviser,
Mason, hewer or crafty quarrier,
For every wright and passing carpenter
That may be found, either far or near;
For such as couldë gravë, grope[1] or carve,
Or such as weren able for to serve
With lime or stonë, for to raise a wall
With batailling and crestës martial,
Or such as haddë cunning in their head,
Alabaster, either white or red
Or marble gray for to polish it plain,
To make it smooth of veinës and of grain.
He sent also for every imager
Both in entaille,[2] and every portrayer
That couldë drawe, or with colour paint
With hewës freshë, that the work not faint;
And such as could with countenances glad
Make an imagë that will never fade,
To counterfeit in metal, tree or stone
The subtle workë of Pigmaleoun,
Or of Appollo,[3] the which as bookës tell
In imagery all other did excel,
For by his crafty working curious
The tomb he made of King Darius."[4]

These words describe, with no more than natural poetic licence, what we have seen Lydgate's patron Henry VI doing, a generation after the lines were written, at Eton and King's College. Moreover, bishops and city councils must have done much the same, according to their powers, when those vast cathedrals were built which surpassed even the great monastic churches in magnificence and in haste of execution. Monk, citizen and prince are all combining to fan the flame of Gross-Industrie in the building art.

For work on this scale, both in size and in haste,

---

[1] Carve deep and hollow, as the French use the word *fouiller*.
[2] Sculpture.
[3] Apelles; cf. Chaucer, *Wife of Bath's Prologue*.
[4] *Troy Book*, E.G.T.S., extra series, 1906, vol. i, p. 138 (probably written somewhere about 1410).

necessarily created the contract system. St. Antonino of Florence, writing about 1420, speaks of it as a growing practice ;¹ but it was the princes of Italy, and especially the popes, who made it quite normal a generation later.

Traces, of course, may be found much earlier. Quicherat has published the analysis of a document of 1261 which shows distinct traces of modernity. The abbot of St.-Gilles in Languedoc, backed up by the *operarius*—i.e. the monk who supervises this part of the abbey business and revenues—makes a contract with Martin, a master-mason of Vauvert. Master Martin undertakes to order, devise, and direct the building work, to decide what must be bought, and to keep watch over the supplies. For his trouble, he takes 100 *sols tournois* [equivalent to £1 5s. sterling of then English money] at Pentecost, as the equivalent of a suit of clothes. In addition, he gets a wage of two sols for every work-day on which he commences before midday. He can claim, any day of the year, food for himself and his horse. If he chooses to eat outside, he takes the ration of two monks in bread and wine.² If he prefers to eat in the abbey, he will sit at the abbot's table, or in his absence, at that of the prior or of the judge, but only on non-fast days ; and then his portion shall be that of a monk, valued at three deniers.³ On fast days, he will fetch from the kitchen " a monk's *generale* and pittance," a phrase which Quicherat glosses, on what seem far-fetched and doubtful grounds, as " half as much again as a monk's fast-diet." This master-mason evidently intended to live only the summer months at St.-Gilles ; for the agreement binds him, for the period between Martinmas and Whitsuntide,

---

¹ *Summa Major*, pars. iii, tit. viii, cap. 4, § 8.

² Doubled, as we shall presently see, to make up for his missing all victuals except bread and wine.

³ Twelve *deniers* went to the *sol*; this, therefore, would be ¾d. of contemporary English money. But this valuation apparently comprised only the two dishes ; the bread and wine, accounted for elsewhere, being here omitted.

" to come with all speed whensoever anything unexpected occurs in the course of the works, if he is sent for by the abbot or the *operarius*."

Much nearer to the modern contract is the indenture for the construction of Fotheringhay Church, made in 1434–5, between the representatives of the Duke of York and William Horwood, freemason, of Fotheringhay. This indenture system had already become common in war. Our armies were regularly thus organized in the Hundred Years' War, after the earlier tentative stages. A certain great captain would bind himself by indenture to supply the king with so many men, at so much per man and per day, according to a regular tariff.[1] This captain would then often indent with minor captains, each of whom undertook to bring a certain quota at a certain price ; and these, again, might raise their quotas by indenting with smaller men. The Italians, the great business men of that day, were doing the same. Long ago, in the crusade of 1204, the Venetians had entered into a regular business contract with the Crusaders. In 1337, again, Ayton Doria of Genoa contracted in regular form with the King of France. He was to supply twenty war-galleys, fully equipped and manned, at the rate of 900 gold florins per month and per ship. The king accepted forty galleys at that rate, and used them for four months ; this bargain cost him 144,000 florins, a sum equivalent to the whole budget of one of the great medieval Hanse cities.[2] Sombart's comment upon this and similar incidents runs : " It was war which created the Stock Exchange."

But a princely baron like the Duke of York very naturally carried his military experience into his business at home. He indented to raise a church as he might have indented to raise a division for Agincourt, in which battle he lost his life. We must not exaggerate the

[1] For example, the indenture of the Earl of Kent with Edward III in 1360 (Rymer, *Foedera*, vol. iii, 1825, p. 510).

[2] Sombart, K.K., pp. 33, 51, 65.

connexion of ideas ; it may well be that building contracts in similar form were drawn up long before this
surviving contract for Fotheringhay. We must not
exaggerate, but neither must we ignore the fact that the
same movement may be traced in both fields, and that
it would be natural for each to influence the other.
After giving, in great detail, the size and description of
the new nave and tower required, even down to such
small items as the mouldings, the contract proceeds :
" And of all the work that in this same indenture is
devised and rehearsed [i.e. nave and tower], my said Lord
of York shall find the carriage and stuff ; that is to say,
lime, stone, sand, ropes, bolts, ladders, timber, scaffolds,
gynnes [*machinery*], and all manner of stuff that be-
longeth to the said work ; for which work, well, truly
and duly to be made and finished in wise as it is before
devised and declared, the said William Horwood shall
have of my said Lord £300 sterling ; of the which sum
he shall be paid in wise as it shall be declared hereafter.
That is to say, when he hath taken his ground [*laid the
foundation*] of the said kirk, aisles, buttresses, porch and
steeple, hewn and set his ground-table-stones, and his
ligements [i.e. string-courses] and the wall thereunto
within and without, as it ought to be well and duly made,
then he shall have £6 13s. 4d. And when the said William
Horwood hath set one foot above the ground-table-
stone, as well throughout the outer side as the inner side
of the said work, then shall he have payment of £100
sterling.[1] And so for every foot of the said work, after
that it be fully wrought and set, as it ought to be, and as
it is afore devised, till it come to the full height of the
highest of the finials and battlement of the said body,
hewing, setting and raising . . . [*sic*] of the steeple, after
it be passed the highest of the embattlement of the said
body, he shall have but xxxs sterlings till it be fully ended
and performed, in wise as it is before devised." Here,
then, all is calculated on a general scale ; five pounds for

[1] The copyist seems to have mistaken C^{li} for C^s.

every foot in height up to the battlements, and thenceforward, nothing being left to raise but the tower, only thirty shillings a foot.[1] The contract was stringent in other directions also. " During all the said work the said Will. Horwood shall neither set more nor fewer freemasons, rough-setters nor layers thereupon, but such as shall be ordained to have the governance and oversight of the said work under my Lord of York will ordain him and assign him to have. And if so be that the said Will. Horwood make not full payment of all or any of his workmen, then the clerk of the work shall pay him in his presence, and stop as mickle in the said Will. Horwood's hand, as the payment that shall be due unto the workmen cometh to. And during all the said work the setters shall be chosen and taken by such as have the governance and oversight of the said work by my said Lord ; they to be paid by the hand of Will. Horwood . . . . And if so be that the said Will. Horwood will complain and say at any time that the two said setters, or any of them, be not profitable nor sufficient workmen for my Lord's avail, then by oversight of master-masons of the country they shall be deemed ; and if they be found faulty or unable, then they shall be changed, and others taken and chosen in. . . . And if it so be that the said Will. Horwood make not full end of the said work within term reasonable [which shall be specified beforehand] then he shall yield his body to prison at my Lord's will, and all his movable goods and heritages at my said Lord's disposition and ordinance." [2]

It will be noted that we have in this indenture another definitely modern feature ; a specified penalty for breach

[1] Compare this with Dunmow Priory, where in 1533 the monks paid a mason for $9\frac{1}{2}$ feet of steeple which he had built for them; the price was £11 os. 7d. (V. C. H. Essex, vol. ii, p. 153).

[2] Dugdale-Caley, vol. vi, pp. 1414 ff. For other contracts, besides those noted in Prof. A. Hamilton Thompson's Med. Build. Docts., p. 19, see Brutails, pp. 26–7, 54, 74 ; Kirby Muxloe (bricks laid at 1s. 6d. per thousand). Portions of Westminster Abbey were done by " task-work " from 1253 onwards.

of contract. This occurs much earlier, in a document which I have printed elsewhere.[1] Among the muniments of the Cistercian abbey of Dunes, in Flanders, is a contract of about A.D. 1200 with a hired scribe. He is to finish a book in as good letters as the specimen which he had begun ; he undertakes to do no other work till this is finished ; if he breaks this promise, he shall be " kept in prison and in iron bonds . . . never to go forth until the said work shall have been altogether completed. . . . And, for the keeping of the aforesaid articles, the said [scribe] hath pledged [to his employer], by his faith, his own person and heirs, and all his goods, whether movable or immovable, present or future, without right of appeal to any tribunal outside the bishop's court." And, naturally, this fixing of a definite sanction for the contract became more and more general, though, equally naturally, the crude resource of imprisonment was replaced by a money-penalty, as society became more civilized. This comes out clearly in the arrangements of Henry VII's executors for the completion of King's College Chapel. Here, though the contracts are not yet in quite the stringent modern form, yet they mark a definite stage between ordinary medieval small-business and the capitalistic Gross-Industrie of to-day. The master-masons engage to finish the work at the rate of £100 per bay ; on the other hand, one " binds himself, his heirs and executors, in £300 of good and lawful money of England," for the due performance of his part. The four master-glaziers who first contracted for the windows were to receive 16d. per foot, and bound themselves in 500 marks for performance of the job. The two to whom this contract was transferred accepted it under bond of £200. It is evident that all these artists were also capitalistic contractors.[2]

But let us go back to illustrate Fotheringhay, perhaps

[1] *Social Life in Britain*, p. 102.

[2] Willis and Clark, vol. i, pp. 610, 616, 618. For another contract see *Gould*, vol. i, p. 304.

the most interesting of all our contracts, from the generalizations of St. Antonino, who at that same moment was working and writing in Florence. There, capitalism and the Gross-Industrie were more advanced than in England, and there is a very modern ring in the Saint's advice to confessors for dealing with the men of business whose souls they were directing. He is treating now of " architects or builders "—*de architectis seu aedificatoribus.* After the uncomplimentary passage which I have quoted earlier, tracing back this art to Cain and Nimrod, two of the least respectable among all Old Testament figures in medieval tradition, he notes that the holy patriarchs were content to live in tents, " knowing that they had here no continuing city, but expecting a house not made with hands, a most spacious house in heaven." He then goes on to specify the ordinary artisan's temptations to idleness or dishonest work, and finally deals with what we may call the contractor. " If men are paid by the yard for the building they do, the employer supplying them with all the materials, then they commit fraud if, for the sake of doing more work and earning more, they work not properly but carelessly, whereby the building is rendered feeble and unprofitable. Thirdly, when they undertake to construct a building at their own expense, supplying all the materials for a certain price specified between builder and employer, then they sometimes cheat by not putting lime enough, or not supplying other things in their right place, in order that they may spend less of the stuff which it is their part to supply, whereby the building is rendered insufficient. Nor could they be excused on the plea that, if they chose to supply what is agreed upon, and to labour diligently, then they would earn very little, so small is the sum that they receive ; for it is their duty to take heed hereunto at the outset ; but they do this in order that they may get the job rather than other men."[1]

This brings us to the most important stage of the

[1] *Summa Major*, pars. iii, tit. viii, c. 4, § 8.

evolution which we are tracing. Two generations before these princely executors put the Cambridge work into the hands of capitalists, the same stage had been reached in Italy, and especially at Rome. The old medieval system no longer sufficed for this rush of enormous and costly buildings ; the patriarchal and personal methods of earlier centuries must now give way to something like the methods of the modern joint-stock company. In the Middle Ages, the master of the works had hired workmen for the job ; had bought the materials (it was a step forward when, as at St.-Gilles, not he but the contracting master-mason was responsible for those materials) ; had put all these ingredients, so to speak, to simmer together ; and from this caldron the complete building had finally emerged. Even at King's College, where the executors were dealing with masons and glaziers who possessed considerable capital, and who could contract to turn the building out at so much per bay, so much per turret, so much per pinnacle, these capitalist head-workmen did not supply the materials. It was left to the great princes of the Continent to arrive at this final stage of commercialization. The earlier part of this story is brought out by Müntz,[1] and the later by Sombart.[2] The movement had begun in the earlier fifteenth century ;[3] but quite definite is the contract between Paul II and Bernardo di Lorenzo for building the palace and church of San Marco at Rome, a contract repeated almost verbally from a previous agreement of Pius II with Bernardo's predecessors. And now, writes Müntz, " an attentive study of the contract . . . which we have had copied from the secret archives of the Vatican, permits us to go still farther and to assert that Bernardo [and his three partners] participated in the building of the Palace of San Marco not as architects but as plain contractors. In fact, they pledge themselves,

[1] *Les arts à la cour des Popes*, II (1879), pp. 20, 25, 52, 55, 290.
[2] *M.K.*, pp. 773 ff.
[3] Müntz, I (1878), 46 ff., 104 ff., 157 ff., 164, 169.

for a flat rate of 19 *grossi* for each yard of masonry, to dig the foundations, raise the walls, and so on. The notary, at every point, takes care to mark that these works are to be done in conformity with measures given to the contractors. Does not this seem to prove that the plans were drawn by others ? Nothing is more frequent, in the fifteenth century, than this sort of agreement. Thus, in the reign of Nicholas V, Beltramo di Martino, of Varese, had undertaken to rebuild the gallery of St. Peter's, under penalty for failure. Under Paul II, similar contracts are equally abundant. At San Marco itself we see two artists, far more celebrated than the preceding, helping as plain contractors ; these are Giuliano da San Gallo, and Theo del Caprino. Giuliano (or, as our documents call him, Julianus son of Francis of Florence), seems to have been specially charged with the masonry. Theo, on the contrary, with a large number of other ' stone-cutters,' was busy with cutting the blocks of travertine needed for the building. He received nineteen [soldi] of Bologna per ell. Sometimes, however, we find him doing more interesting work ; window-frames, marble fire-places, and so on. But (it will be said), if such eminent artists consented to work like plain artisans, sometimes at task-work and sometimes at day-work, then they must have had, above them, some very eminent chief ; a master of imposing genius ; how, then, can this master's name have remained unknown ? That name is no longer a secret for my readers. I have shown that, in March 1466, Giacomo da Pietra-Santa figured among the witnesses of the contract signed with Bernardo di Lorenzo. . . . Shall we be accused of rashness if we identify him with, we need not say the architect, but one of the architects of San Marco ? "

On a previous page, Müntz writes : " The number of supervisors of the works at San Marco (*superstites*, *præsidentes*) seems at the first glance so considerable that we can scarcely understand how all this multiplicity failed to hinder the regularity of the pope's enterprises.

But, if we note the pecuniary situation of the different employés, and not merely their title, we soon find that there was very great inequality between them. Those who received ten florins a month were evidently above those who took only two. The former were real head-architects ; the others were simple overseers, foremen, or accountants." He proceeds to show that nearly all the artists recorded in the account-rolls are North Italians, or even Germans ; scarcely any were Romans, or from Roman territory in the wider sense. He then continues : " At San Marco, and probably also at the Vatican and at St. Peter's, the following system was employed. The work in gross was undertaken under a separate agreement with a company of contractors and architects ; the secondary work was done sometimes by the task, sometimes by the day [the wages ranged from 18 *Bolognesi* for the best master-masons, to 4 for the lowest labourers]. The orders for payment are generally collective ; but it does not seem that the workmen were divided into squads, as Filareto supposed. In fact, the number comprised in the same order varies almost with every payment. Take, for instance, the payments made to the German master Giovanni di Pietro ; once, beyond his own wages, he draws those of four labourers ; another time, the wages of eleven ' fellow-wallers and stone-cutters,' and of twenty-two labourers. This last mention shows that the masons were not even always separated from the stone-cutters."[1]

Worldly princes followed this same course, in proportion as their revenues and their circumstances permitted ; the Field of the Cloth of Gold was a natural sequel to this Renaissance display in Rome and under the richer

---

[1] Something like this seems to emerge from the Bodmin accounts ; at least two different " fellowships " are mentioned, but their membership seems to vary. (See Appendix 11.) It looks as though the smaller men worked, on a precarious tenure, under the others ; and it may go some way to support my explanation of unsigned stones (chap. viii). For farther notice of the advance of these popes towards modern Gross-Industrie, see Müntz, 1878, pp. 84, n. 3 and 104.

despots of Italy. At the moment when Paul II was building his magnificent palaces, in 1468, Charles the Bold celebrated his wedding at Bruges. One hundred and thirty-seven painters and carvers were employed . . . "They were called in from Tournai, Brussels, and Antwerp, from Hainault, from Cambrai and Arras, Valenciennes and Douai, Louvain and Ypres. As Hugo van der Goes was of the number, mingled among the rest without distinction, we cannot believe that they were mere daubers."[1] Their work for this one festivity totalled at least 983 days. Jacques Daret, " maistre peintre," received 24 *sols* a day ; the lowest pay was 5½ and the average was 12 *sols*, 1½ *deniers*. Special account is taken of the expenses of an artist who spent six days going and coming and " riding round to Ghent and Audenarde and other good towns, to fetch in all the best workmen of the country, both painters and others."[2] All this was only the logical consequence of the pressgang exercised by medieval princes here and there from early times ; but the fact that Gross-Industrie was now growing so much more frequent implied a real social change. And, as Sombart notices, it began first with the popes, masters of vast wealth from the taxation of Christendom, and with the despotic princes of Italy and Flanders, who again had specially rich sources of taxation. Thence it spread to France and Spain ; only later did it reach England.[3] Moreover, it was very naturally associated with the recrudescence of slavery in the later Middle Ages. In Italy, that system had never died out altogether ; it revived very much with the growth of commerce and luxury ; there were slaves at Rome, real slaves in the Carolina plantation sense, until almost modern times. In 1310, a systematic raid is

[1] A. Michiels, *Hist. de la peinture flamande et hollandaise*, vol. ii, p. 260. A very interesting account of Prof. Cartellieri's fuller and more recent studies on this subject in *The Times Lit. Sup.*, February 1, 1923, p. 69.

[2] Ibid., 417.

[3] *L.K.*, pp. 78–91.

recorded to have brought 12,000 slaves into the Italian market; in 1355, another raid brought 7,000. However we may discount medieval figures, this is quite characteristic of that commercialization of society which was one factor in the Renaissance. Sombart specifies the slave-traders in chronological order; the commerce began first with Jews, then the Venetians took it up, then the Genoese, then the Portuguese; last came the French and the English.[1] In most European countries, the ancient Roman slave had gradually become a medieval serf, and the serf was becoming a free man; the Italian Renaissance harked back here, as elsewhere, to the traditions of Pagan Rome.[2]

[1] *L.K.*, p. 148.

[2] See an article on this subject in *The Review of the Churches* for July 1927, and de Gourmont, *l.c.*, p. 147: "The Roman popes made Rome into the twin capital of Christendom and of Paganism."

CHAPTER XXIV

RENAISSANCE AND CONSTRUCTION.—(2)

SO much for the extent to which the Renaissance brought us on to Gross-Industrie through the contract system. But, as Sombart points out, this is not all ; it brought us onward also to modern methods of standardization. The movement in this direction was inevitable ; architecture and its ancillary arts could not become a Gross-Industrie without some considerable advance in the standardization of materials.

Some things, of course, were standardized in very early times. Here, again, war provided a stimulus. A " sheaf " of arrows seems to have meant something definite from the first time we find the word mentioned ; and Sombart traces military standardization down to its final perfection under Louis XIV. In the building arts, nails were very early standardized, to some extent at least. The still surviving phrase " tenpenny nail " marks a time when nails of the largest size ran at tenpence per hundred. Into the art (we may call it) of writing, the Universities introduced definite standardization ; a *pecia* contained 16 columns, each consisting of 62 lines, with 32 letters to the line.[1] Two *peciae* made a *quaternio*, from which we get *quire*, the French *cahier*, and the well-known poem of " The King's Quair." This standardization may be traced in a rudimentary form from about 1300 ; in the fifteenth century it was so definite that it was incorporated in the University

---

[1] Wattenbach, *Schriftwesen im M.A.*, Leipzig, 1896, p. 185 ; cf. H. Rashdall. *Univs. of Europe*, I, 191 ff., 415 ff.

statues of Bologna and Padua.[1] This, of course, must not be taken too literally in practice; here as with all medieval statutes and medieval measures, we must allow for considerable variations; yet the standardization was so much of a reality that Savigny is able to quote a MS. of the late thirteenth or early fourteenth century in which the whole book is transformed—it may be said also, deformed—by the scribe's exact reckoning of his *peciae*. "Each part consists of 24 *peciae*, so that the whole runs to 48; and in fact this is noted at the beginning and end: ' here begins ' (or ' ends ') ' the 1st *pecia* of the 1st part,' and so on. For most of these *peciae* he does in fact take half a *quaternus*, or four pages; but, since the *pecia* mostly comes to an end before these four pages are filled, he leaves the rest blank; indeed, more than once he leaves a whole blank leaf, which is then cut away." The universities did much also to standardize book prices, both new and second-hand.

But it was a combination of military requirements and of luxury that produced one of the earliest instances of standardization in architecture, and probably the most striking instance until we come to these popes of the full Renaissance.

Sombart is probably right in picking out Avignon as the first " modern " princely court, the definite predecessor of the Milanese court, or of Fontainebleau under Francis I.[2] If the visitor will take a tape-measure with him to that enormous fortress-palace of Avignon, built almost entirely within about twenty-two years (1336–1358), he will find that every stone within his reach, on the wall-surface, is of exactly the same thickness. The official curator of the building has assured me that this

---

[1] F. C. v. Savigny, *Gesch. d. röm. Rechts im M.A.*, 2nd ed., vol. iii, pp. 580 ff. In Peterhouse Library, several fifteenth century MSS. have the scribal prices noted at the end; calculation shows that there was a recognized rate of so much per word or per letter.

[2] Compare the details given by G. Mollat, *Les Papes d'Avignon*, 1st ed., p. 348.

rule has scarcely any exception throughout that mountain of masonry. Many hundreds of workmen, therefore, were employed during these twenty-two years in cutting these innumerable stones to one exact standard; only thus could the layers have laid at double rate, and the popes have satisfied their feverish haste to finish the building. It must have been almost as great an innovation, in its way, as when Louis XIV set his army of builders to work on day and night shifts, so that there was no moment of repose, at his palace of Versailles.[1] Later in the same century, we get similar evidence, though naturally on a smaller scale, from Troyes Cathedral. The masons were ordered to supply fifty stones of three feet in length, a hundred of two-and-a-half, and fifty of two feet; the whole two hundred to have a uniform height and breadth of one foot.[2] A century later, there was evidently still more standardization at Bordeaux. There were ordinarily three classes of stones : (1) *queyrons*, *doublerons* or *demi-pierres*, measuring $1 \times 1 \times 1$ foot; (2) *pierres*, 2 feet by 1 foot, and (3) *grandes-pierres* of irregular dimensions.[3] The first two classes were bought at a recognized market price per hundred or per thousand.

And, earlier than this, we find even sculpture being sold by the foot. In 1447, the Hotel de Ville of Béthune was burned down, and the municipality set themselves to replace it by a structure worthy of their civic prosperity. They commissioned a painter to make " two portraitures or devices " of the building, and paid him £5 for " the labour and subtilty therein expended." They chose the design which seemed most suitable ; and then, " shortly afterwards, the mason-work of the building was adjudged to Jehan Wiot, mason and carver

---

[1] *L.K.*, p. 115.

[2] Quicherat, II, 198.

[3] Brutails, p. 72 ; cf. 59, 69–71, 88 ff. Nails were still more definitely standardized ; ibid., p. 91. The Xanten, Eton, Bodmin and Adderbury accounts seem to imply something like the same standardization in the fifteenth century.

in hard sandstone, for the sum of £693, while Amand
Millon demanded £198 for the carpentry-work. Wiot,
under cross-examination by the master of the works [i.e.
the business representative of the municipality, like the
operarius of St.-Gilles], declared that, apart from ordinary
wall-stones, he would need for the lower courses xx feet
of soeulles, listeaux, planques and steps for winding
stairs, at 18*d*. the foot.[1] For the encaulements, he said,
xxiii white stones will be needed, parpains of 2½ feet and
3 feet, from the Bouvignies quarry, at 2*s*. 6*d*. ; while the
xiii white stones, also called parpains, which have been
furnished by Jehan Pinchon, master-mason to my lord
Duke of Burgundy at his castle of Hesdin, will serve for
the borderings of white stone, for the pavillons and for
the boss-work. The five tabernacles at the angles, with
mouldings or leaf-work, whereon the arms of several
lords will be carved, and the pinnacles surmounting their
canopies will need white stone, freestone of Lille [*franques
pierres de Lille*] ; four, at £4, will suffice for one tabernacle. Note also that each tabernacle, canopy included,
will cost £18."

It was natural that this standardization of art should
begin in this most highly-commercialized corner of
Europe, where literature also was organized into a trade
as it was organized nowhere else. But, a few generations
later, we find even England estimating her statuary by
the foot-rule. Here is an extract from the estimate of
about 1515 for King's College Chapel :

" Two images of kings at the west door in two tabernacles made for the same, either of 8 feet high. Four at
the south and north doors of the said church, either of
6 foot high ; and 48 Images within the said church,
every of them of three foot high. Amounting in all to
172 foot, at 5*s*. the foot, esteemed in workmanship,

---

[1] There must be an error here ; probably the MS. has XXc—i.e. 2,000,
which at 18*d*. the foot would cost £150. So also with the XXIII and
XIII directly after. I am obliged to leave several words untranslated ;
but this does not affect the document as an illustration of method.

which amounteth unto £43. Forty ton of Yorkshire stone is esteemed to be sufficient for all the said Images. At 6 shillings 8*d.* the ton, £13 6*s.* 8*d.*" [1]

About the same time, we find a farther standardization of materials. Glass was imported in standard quantities from Normandy and Rhineland ; it was reckoned, as arrows were, by the sheaf.[2]   And artist glaziers undertook, not only at King's but elsewhere, to produce painted windows at so much per foot. In 1477–8, tiles were standardized in England by Act of Parliament ; there are exact specifications for all sorts of tiles, with heavy fines for contravention.[3]

With this same movement, came a similar growth of taste for symmetry, in contrast with the irregularities which delight our modern eyes so much in medieval work. Not but that the Middle Ages themselves had sought symmetry, and had often been driven by mere necessity to the inequalities that we love in them. The great trade-halls of Bruges and Ypres were already far on the way to modern standardization. Again, French antiquaries have long emphasized the remarkable growth of new towns in the south and the centre, especially during the thirteenth century ; towns which may very commonly be distinguished by their very names, as Villeneuve, Villefranche, La Bastide.[4] These were often built upon a plan almost as regular as a Roman camp or a new American town, and for much the same business

---

[1] Willis and Clark, vol. i, p. 482.

[2] E.g. *Test. Eborac*, vol. iv, Surtees Soc., 1868, p. 334 (1508 A.D.) ; the *York Fabric Rolls* supply similar evidence. The movement may be traced in every industry ; at York, in 1420, the price for chipping bows was 1*s.* 4*d.* per 100 ; for boring horns, 1*s.* 3*d.* per 1,000 (*York Memo. Book*, Surtees Soc., 1912, vol. i, p. 48).

[3] Statute of 17 Ed. IV, chap. iv.   See Appendix 32.

[4] A very interesting summary of these researches, with added matter, has been printed by Prof. T. F. Tout (*Medieval Town Planning*, Manchester Univ. Press, 1*s.* 6*d.*). The French articles may be found in *Annales archéologiques*, vol. vi, pp. 71 ff. and 302 ff. ; xi, 335 ff. ; xii, 24 ff. ; xiv, 361 ff.

reasons. The business then was military; here, again, it was war that stimulated men to something more elaborately mechanical, and therefore more standardized, than the village or the town had ever become so long as it had been left to automatic development. And here, again, luxury worked strongly for the same subordination of individual choice to a regularized collective plan. The utility of fortification and the architectural taste of the princely patron pointed in one and the same direction; both required greater and more uniform masses of masonry. Before Charles V had swept away the thousand pleasing irregularities of what may be called a great abbey-village at Ghent, in favour of half a dozen uniform smooth bastions, popes had begun to do much the same for their own city. " Early in the fifteenth century the modern spirit, so methodical in all things and so fond of straight lines, began to manifest itself in the cutting of spacious streets through the ruins and rambling habitations of the city. By a bull dated March 30, 1425, Martin V re-established the office of the commissioners of streets (magistri viarum). [Eugenius IV, Nicholas V, Paul II, Sixtus IV, and Alexander VI followed the same policy.] It cannot be denied that these improvements in the material aspect and welfare of the city involved great losses on the archæological and historical side. . . . Follow Poggio Bracciolini in his ride through the city in 1447, the year of the election of Nicholas V. Beginning with the Capitol, Poggio describes the southern platform of the hill, where the Caffarelli palace now stands, as covered with the colossal remains of the temple of Jupiter; but a few decades later columns, capitals, and frieze had disappeared so completely that archæologists since then have found serious difficulty in determining which of the two summits of the hill was occupied by the Capitolium and which by the Citadel."[1]

Finally, even ordinary noblemen, when they were rich or extravagant enough, followed the example of their

[1] Lanciani, *l.c.*, p. 204.

betters. A wave of semi-modern standardization swept over the French castles ; where the baron could not afford to pull down and rebuild altogether, he did his

THE CASTLE OF BURY (LOIR-ET-CHER)

best to reduce it to the same sort of regularity which it pleased the popes to impose upon the Roman streets. Viollet-le-Duc, in one of his inimitable illustrative sketches, has shown how this process was applied to the château of Bury. The great towers were gutted from top to bottom, and then fitted with a uniform set of windows for domestic convenience. True, these are far more beautiful than the modern sash window usually is ; but the slippery slope is evident ; and we may see how far the material requirements of the Renaissance, the demands of fortification or of growing comfort or of wider industry and commerce and culture, impelled men to constructions which threw into the shade, even when they did not directly involve the destruction of, much that our present generation would most have prized in the art of earlier centuries.

This, and a good deal more if this be not enough, may be urged in answer to Mâle's plea that Protestantism, not Renaissance, killed Gothic art. For the Renaissance was an earlier, a deeper and a wider movement than Protestantism ; in one not unreal sense, it was the mother of Protestantism. It was a complex current fed by many side-streams that tended all in the same direction ; indeed, a current so strong that it swept nearly all the minor currents of its time into that direction. Everything, in the sixteenth century, thus conspired to one general end, the making of a new world. And, of this general revolution, English Protestantism was in many ways among the most conservative currents. Elizabethan and Jacobean domestic architecture remained still Gothic in its general principles. Scarcely any new churches were built, indeed, because the old had long been there, and were still preserved at least as carefully as in any other land, more carefully than in most. Yet, even so, a certain amount of new work was built in the true Gothic spirit. The construction of Bath Abbey Church was continued after the medieval design all through Elizabeth's reign ; and the whole was consecrated under James I. John Williams, Bishop of Lincoln, built a real Gothic library at St. John's College, Cambridge, in 1624 ;

and the great entrance-hall of Christ Church, Oxford, was even later. Yet all this time, and through succeeding generations, Continental orthodox authorities were destroying Gothic work at a rate which was scarcely limited except by the limits of their purse. The Abbey of Cîteaux, mother of the whole Cistercian Order, would have been entirely rebuilt in the style in which one great existing wing was built, if only the Revolution had not come and put an end to farther vandalism. To realize the devastation wrought thus in the French monasteries, we must look through the splendid collection of bird's-eye views of all the abbeys of the congregation of St.-Maur, made about 1690 and published in 1871 by M. Peigné-Delacourt under the title of *Monasticon Gallicanum*. The churches, it is true, had in most cases been spared ; but, of the rest of the abbey buildings, more than half had been rebuilt in some more modern barrack-style. In South Germany and Austria, even more destruction had been wrought. At the same moment at which the Bishop of Lincoln was building St. John's College library, the monks of the great abbey of Admont rebuilt their whole monastery with the exception of the precinct wall, which, as an outlying feature devoted to mere utility, was suffered to partly retain its ancient medieval character. The contemporary engraving of this building, and of the tomb of the saintly founder, substituted at the same time for the old Gothic tomb, are, after all, entirely in keeping with other examples more easily accessible and far too numerous for rehearsal here. I need only instance the whole of the great abbey buildings at St. Gallen, or the orthodox ornamentation applied to the choir arches at Chartres Cathedral and at St.-Maclou-de-Rouen. And this same contrast may be traced down to the present day.[1] Modern French Gothic churches are, almost without exception, inferior to those built at the same date in England.

[1] This is clearly brought out in Montalembert's monograph on " Vandalism and Catholicism in Art " (*Œuvres*, vol. vi, 1861). See Appendix 33.

Their stained glass is scarcely ever tolerable, and generally of a vileness beyond all description. Their furniture, and especially the machine-made imagery turned out from the shops round St.-Sulpice at Paris, has become a byword even among the orthodox. One architect of real talent, a man far beyond his time, Pugin, was mainly converted to Roman Catholicism by his dislike of the current Protestant architecture of the early nineteenth century ; but, once within the fold, he was accustomed to confess bitter disappointment.[1] The new Cathedral at Westminster, with all its striking qualities, does not pretend to be Gothic ; indeed, the absence of any such pretence is among its most striking qualities. It is difficult to understand how anyone familiar with both English and Continental buildings can, after carefully weighing all the evidence, seriously contend that Protestantism was the true destroyer of Gothic art.

[1] See Appendix 34.

CHAPTER XXV

CONCLUSION

IT seems impossible, in face of the facts, to believe in a past age in which a large body of men worked as religious artists (in the full modern sense of both terms, *art* and *religion*) upon a series of monuments which succeeding ages have been able only to destroy or to caricature. The vast majority of masons either did not possess, or had no opportunity of developing, more artistic sense than that of the modern skilled mechanic. A small minority were not only stone-dressers but also stone-carvers ; yet these were probably no more numerous, in proportion to population, than the exhibitors at our art galleries of to-day. Moreover, even of this minority only a small fraction showed real originality. " The artists of the fifteenth century imitated with almost the same docility as those of the twelfth. Imitation is still the great law of [medieval] art. . . . There were a few artists, at the end of the fourteenth century and during the fifteenth, who were able to invent. . . . But the illumination of service-books was as much an industry as an art. The head of the workshop alone was a real artist ; he alone took the liberty of making discreet innovations."[1] Those words might as truly have been written about stone-carving as about illumination. Again, the extent to which glass-painters copied each other and repeated themselves has long been recognized. " Moreover, it is a popular fallacy that the medieval glass-painter was a sentimentalist, a man of high ideals, who worked chiefly for the love of God's Church and its adornment, and to that end was content to labour

[1] Mâle, II, 71 ; cf. Cennini, introd., pp. 16, 18.

479

for very small wages. In reality this was far from being the case."[1]

We are apt to forget sometimes that the great period of Gothic art in England, from the Conquest to the Reformation, covers four centuries and a half, or a considerably longer period than that which divides the Reformation from the present day. We are surveying, therefore, the aggregate results of fifteen generations of medieval work; or rather, we survey what time has spared from those four hundred and fifty years. In England, where so many monasteries lived on as cathedrals, and the parish churches have been comparatively respected, we have still perhaps a quarter of what was standing in 1530, especially if we count the fragments; for instance, a single bay of a cloister often enables us to judge of the rest. In France and in Italy, a larger proportion of medieval work has perished, and more, perhaps, by rebuilding than by revolution. If so much has survived anywhere, this is due mainly to a peculiar product of modern civilization, the antiquarian sense. It would scarcely be an exaggeration to say that the Gothic work of the thirteenth century has seldom found such a terrible enemy as it had in the Gothic builders of the later Middle Ages. Medieval art, like the French Revolution, " devoured its own children."

Let us, therefore, temper our regrets, though regrets there must always be. Something has certainly been lost, partly or wholly, of those factors which made for the greatness of medieval painting and sculpture. There was in those days a sense of unity in purpose, and a patriarchal simplicity of intercourse between man and man, which we must do what we can to recapture. But those who feel this most strongly seem least able to tell us how it is to be achieved. Much of what charms us in the past is due to the simplicity of comparative inexperience, the naturally childlike mind. But it would

[1] J. D. le Couteur, *English Medieval Painted Glass*, S.P.C.K., 1926, p. 18, cf. L. F. Salzman, *Med. Eng. Industries*, Oxford, 1923, p. 309.

seem almost a contradiction in terms to aim consciously at simple inexperience; and, in fact, those who lash their flanks to be childlike are too often merely childish. Nor does the gild system seem a real remedy, unless we are content to take it with all its apparently inseparable limitations. A socialist society could doubtless suppress all really bad art but only at the expense of a great deal that is best. There are certain sides of the art of a man like Jean-François Millet which a medieval carver would never have been fully free to develop except in caricature.

Therefore, while repudiating pusillanimous content with things as they are, and while refusing to believe that whatever exists is therefore right, must we not yet accept a great deal of what we deplore, for the present at least, as an almost inevitable consequence of changes which we cannot reverse? Changes, moreover, which, after weighing both sides carefully, we would no more wish to reverse than we wish to go back to the nursery? One mere schoolboy experience struck to me a clear note of warning which constantly sounds again amid speculations in social history. Our village furniture-dealer in Essex, after selling a fine rapier with bullion-gold tassels to an older schoolfellow, and precious fragments of fifteenth-century glass to me from the Bishop of London's palace at Much Hadham, pressed upon us a pair of leather breeches, the last that had ever been seen in the village; a garment which, to his certain knowledge, had been worn for forty consecutive years by a labourer not very long deceased. The leather was almost as stiff as tin; it might have lasted several lives longer, as it had doubt-less lasted several before; but it was a more curious thing to have seen and handled, and to ponder upon at a distance, than to possess. There were volumes of patriarchal poetry in that relic; but who would go back into it? Who can seriously weigh the beautiful thatched cottage, when, as so often, it is insanitary and indecent within, against even the most hideous of those buildings which are helping the modern labourer to live under less degrading conditions ?

For the conditions are less degrading on the whole, even in the towns. Durkheim's *Division du travail social* makes short work of a great deal of nonsense about the noble savage, as compared with his modern descendant. Much as we still need to improve conditions of labour, we must not attempt to go back to the pre-machinery days when every man made for himself whatever he himself wanted. The savage, if he needs a boat, must make it for himself ; if he needs a pair of boots, he must make them. This results not in individual originality, but in its opposite. Take a hundred savages at random ; their separate likes and dislikes resemble each other far more nearly than those of a hundred cotton-operatives, even of those whose daily work is most mechanical. For, during those labour-hours themselves, the modern workman has some time for reflection ; and, when his work is over, he steps out into a world whose variety and whose stimulus differentiates it by a whole horizon from the world of the savage. One will play football, others watch the game, others go to the tavern, or to the public library for a glance at the newspapers ; the hundred Lancashire operatives would show differences of taste quite unknown to the simple savages. Those who complain of modern life as monotonous, and of modern men as lacking in individuality, are superficial observers who mistake one part for the whole. True, we do want to get at the ideal of More's Utopia ; six hours of compulsory breadwork for every man or woman, and not more than six hours for any ; that, if it could be fully carried out, would be enough to get all the world's work done, and would give all men " time to stand and stare." But, while we keep this in view, we must not allow any natural impatience to make us unjust towards certain real lines of past progress, or to stampede us into specious side-avenues which history shows to be blind alleys.

So long as we believe man to be in any sense master

of his destiny, one man's cry of despair is for the rest a
call to action. " From that time forward," writes Mâle
concerning the early sixteenth century, " the Christian
artist had but one resource left : to stand face to face
with the Gospel narrative, and to interpret it as he feels
it." But where is the harm in this ? Have we not here
a change of world-view which, rightly taken, might be
fruitful of still higher art ? May we not answer Mâle
from Goethe's *Faust* ? " If you don't feel it, with all
the pains in the world, you won't get hold of it." Rembrandt thus stood face to face with the Gospel narrative ;
he felt it in many cases more vividly than any medieval
artist ; and his " Raising of Lazarus," apart from its
purely technical excellences, has all the life and the religious feeling of the very best thirteenth century work.
For it was one of the few great deficiencies in that art
that it neglected not only most of the parables but some
of the most striking Gospel scenes, such as : " Suffer ye the
little children to come unto me."   If true religion inevit-
ably expresses itself in true art ; if that is indeed a
universal law which (as we are told) kept Europe straight
for a thousand years ; if from a people's churches, with
their ornaments, the philosophic observer can with
certainty infer that people's faith, why then has there
not grown up a whole school of art capable of impressing
these medievally-neglected things upon the least educated
of our populations ? Is there no need nowadays for a
Bible of the Poor ? Why are the churches filled, so far
as modern art is concerned, with those Stations of the
Cross, and those sickly saint-statues from Paris, which
are a laughing-stock to all art-lovers even among the
orthodox ? There must come a change of heart somewhere ; but where is it to come from ?

It is constantly said that this must come from the
artisan ; we must make a more human being of him, and
then we shall have better art.

By all means ; and, if I thought this present volume
might give legitimate excuse for those who deny or ignore

our duty of doing all we can for the artisan, then it should never have been printed. But is not the problem here very much like the problem of War and Peace? Much can indeed be done by wise measures of detail, but these will be abortive in the long run unless they contribute to a corresponding change of heart.

Let us not forget the fine achievements of the present day at Buckfast Abbey, where the monks have nearly completed a task rare even in the Middle Ages, of building their own church. They have laboured unremittingly for twenty years, never more than six monks, and for most of the time five only; and now the work is almost done. Similar work, I am told, is being done at one spot in America, without denominational religious inspiration, and without encouragement from those who talk loudest about bringing the world back to medieval art; work similar, that is, in organization, though there the workmen are co-operative wage-earners. Such instances must, in the nature of the case, be exceptional; yet they may help us much in the way of example. But how are we to bring back the days in which all workmen worked truly, and had joy in their work, or, at least, had content?

First of all, I should say, by recognizing actual facts. There never was such an age; it is a great exaggeration to imagine it, and those who seek it in the past are wasting precious time and energy. We cannot say they are doing nothing; those also did something who sought the philosopher's stone; but their discoveries would have been far more fruitful if they had built upon a firmer basis of ascertained fact. Nobody would be more astonished and amused than our ancestors of seven centuries ago if they could listen to those who often speak now in their name. From at least the middle of the thirteenth century, when the great Franciscan Berthold of Regensburg was telling his contemporaries from the pulpit what he thought of them, one great theme has been the guile of artisans; their idleness and their shoddy work, except under the strictest supervision. Indeed, from an earlier date than this. Honorius, so-called of Autun, wrote about 1130: succeeding moralists, such as John Gower and St. Antonino of Florence, repeat the same complaints with wearisome emphasis. We must discount what they tell us, but only as we discount the pessimist of our own day.

That, then, seems the first condition; that we should worship the past only where it truly deserves our worship, and that we should blame the present only in so far as it truly falls short of that past. Therefore let us turn away from the journalists who bawl in our ears that this world is a mere Bedlam of feverish competition and dissatisfaction and unrest. Some of us have lived longer than they, and have seen quite as many varieties of human nature, at home and abroad; yet, the older we grow, the more we become aware of, and the deeper respect we feel for, one great class whom these philippics almost ignore; the multitude of good quiet folk who are neither feverish nor over-competitive. Those revivalist preachers are themselves their own fever and pain. Richly paid, they are struggling for more; popular already, they thirst hydroptically for real fame; and their own disquiet gives them this illusion of world-unrest. Meanwhile, millions live on tranquilly in the conviction that man is as much master of his fate as he ever has been; and those millions are the modern analogue of the medieval artisan whom we wish to multiply. They are to be found in all trades and all professions; sometimes they are even masters of some big business. In so far as the medieval artisan was really content with his work and his wage, these men are his true descendants. There is as much honesty and disinterested work now as in the thirteenth century; and, in so far as it can be truly said that the output per man is smaller now, this is mainly due to modern liberty, and to the hesitations which accompany every change, however good in itself. The workman is under far less strict compulsion now, and has far more competing interests. Yet we would not willingly curtail either his liberty or his interests ; let him be free to choose ; let him have the greatest possible variety of choice, even at the risk of his choosing ill. There are very many, unfortunately, who feel their breadwork as drudgery ; and this we must do our best to mend. But these men have nearly always far shorter work-hours than their forefathers ; and, assuming sense and self-control in the man, who shall say that this alternation of drudgery and leisure does not give as fine opportunities, both for self-culture and for public work, as were ever enjoyed by the medieval artisan ? It is lamentable that there should also be so many whose life is drudgery without leisure ; but of this also there was far more in the Middle Ages than we are commonly told. If we can ever arrive at anything near the Utopian proportion of work-hours to leisure, then the problem will probably solve itself *ambulando*, and human nature will find its own balance between work and play. But neither machinery nor the present social structure is a necessary obstacle to this Utopian solution. The problem, it must be repeated, resembles the problem of War and Peace. A world which really desires peace can get it ; a society which really desires six hours of work for all, and no more for any, could arrange that also without abolition of private property and without reducing us all to a general dead level of life.

We possess already, and let us never for a moment forget it, a mass of honest and disinterested work under the most various forms. It is not always organized and gilded ; let us by all means do whatever seems possible to organize it and to give external encouragement. To some extent it is already a conscious and coherent force in our Garden Cities. Plain living and hard thinking are the foundation of success here ; and, if the modern artist is restless, this is often because he is fighting all the while for a far higher wage and wider reputation than that of the medieval artisan. In those days, he was

restricted by circumstances; in the greater freedom of
modern society, he has "chances in life" which his
predecessor had not; and he gambles on those chances.
Yet, again be it said, there are millions who do not thus
bow the knee to Baal, and who are none the less helping
us forward because they are so inconspicuous among us,
and because they accept this world as neither too good
nor too bad for human nature's daily food. They work
and rest, feed and sleep in reasonable content; they
meet other men's eyes frankly and reach out loyally for
other hands, trusting in their fellows and trusting in the
dear old brown earth; and it is these men's seed that
shall inherit the earth. In so far as the medieval craftsman was what William Morris loved to dream of, it is in
such men as this that he survives, and will survive for
ever and ever, through every change of outward form and
every shifting circumstance. The man who knows what
he can do, and is honestly doing it, lives on *sub specie
aeternitatis*.

In painting alone, how many heroes of this kind there
have been in modern times! The old English water-
colour school, and men like Jean-François Millet, have
lived the artist life in a sense of which any age might be
proud. Of J. S. Cotman and David Cox and W. L.
Leitch, to name three almost at random, we have records
worthy of a biographer like Izaak Walton. But, however
many such there may have been or may still be, there
are not yet enough; and the equilibrium of the modern
world is still in one way inferior to that of the thirteenth
century, even when all exaggerations have been cleared
away. Then, a man worked longer hours but could often
take greater pleasure in the work itself; now, the average
artisan has less direct pleasure in his work, and looks more
to relaxation or books outside that work. Even here the
difference is, I believe, far less than is commonly assumed;
the masons and carvers with whom I talked as a boy and
whom I question again nowadays, are not discontented
with their job, nor do they describe their fellows as

discontented. But unquestionably, in the past, there were more masters in a small way; and I must here quote the warning of a wise friend : " It was workman's art, and not sham artists' ' designs ' ' worked out ' by practically slave labour. . . . Then, there was some all-pervading folk-spirit, vitality, story, *a flow of force.* . . . My one little point of anxiety is lest arguers should seize on your facts and say : ' There was no more story, folk-spirit, craft in the Middle Ages than now ; it was always like *this* ; sham Gothic is the same as real Gothic, and Liverpool Cathedral is of the same kind as Lincoln Cathedral. Work was always as hateful as it has now been made with efficiency-movements and stop-watches.' "

I would here venture to amend only two phrases, in the first and in the last sentence. I do not think the words " slave labour " do truly describe the difference between even the commonest modern mason and the men who did the ordinary walling of a medieval church, let alone those who had to standardize the stones for that Avignon palace. And, with regard to modern work, I do think there is another way, a way not merely flattering but essentially true, of looking at the problem.

The nearest modern approach to the folk-spirit of medieval architecture would seem to be in a good many laboratories and machine-shops ; and I believe the analogy to be far closer in this than is generally assumed. I do not speak here only of the great masters of creative work ; men like Pasteur, pursuing his own branch of research " moved, like the even motion of a wheel, by the love that moves the sun and the other stars."[1] and bending daily before the altar in homage to the faith of his birth ; or, on the other hand, Alfred Loisy resolutely facing all the spectres of the past, unmoved by excommunication, intent only upon finding and communicating what he felt to be the truth. Far below these great figures, all through the laboratories and workshops, there are not only thousands who enjoy their

[1] Dante, *Paradiso*, xxxiii, 144.

work, but a select few who take it religiously. They have
the folk-spirit to help them, in this age in which the
very children understand vaguely, and have the keenest
interest in, the working of motor-car and wireless and
aeroplane. Nor are they supported only by this crowd-
interest, as universal as that which existed formerly in
the building arts ; there is also much the same belief,
even to exaggeration, in the value of their industry.
We have nowadays, also, something like the same array
of workers, from the prince or the parson who have
turned aside from their life-job to join the army of in-
ventors, down to Stephenson the peasant and the errand-
boy Edison. There is also much of the same self-sacrifice,
from the heroism of a few who would rather starve than
cease to learn, down to the many who will give up an
extra hour or two for the sake of finishing the job in a
better way ; a sacrifice that is not felt, since in fruitful
labour there is something like the absorbing excitement
of the chase. And, among many who neither consciously
formulate it in their own minds, nor have tongue to talk
of it to others, there is the same uplifting conviction
that this is, in some real sense, a great and sacred work ;
that, since each fresh step reveals so much, and has such
power to rivet the attention, therefore the way itself
must be divine ; that here is one of the many fruitful
paths in this labyrinthine world ; one of those roads
which, however they may twist and turn, lead surely
upwards to the City of God. That feeling is present
even in those who would express it in very different
words ; and a melancholy Jaques among the medieval
masons might well have fathered Mr. Bertrand Russell's
words concerning Pure Mathematics. " Remote from
human passions, remote even from the pitiful facts of
nature, the generations have gradually created an ordered
cosmos, where pure thought can dwell as in its natural
home, and where one, at least, of our nobler impulses
can escape from the dreary exile of the actual world."
At bottom, this is curiously like the answer of St. Catharine

of Siena to those who wondered how she could keep her perpetual serenity amid the drudgery of uncongenial household duties : " I make a little corner of my heart in which I can live with Christ."

Very similar is the artist's problem ; he cannot banish machinery ; he must strive to rise superior to it ; so to use it as not abusing it. There is hope for this and future generations in Mr. Kipling's Scottish engineer.[1]

> " That minds me of our Viscount loon—Sir Kenneth's kin—the chap
> Wi' Russia leather tennis-shoon an' spar-decked yachtin' cap.
> I showed him round last week, o'er all—and at the last says he :
> ' Mister M'Andrews, don't you think steam spoils romance at sea ? '
> Damned ijjit ! I'd been doon that morn to see what ailed The Throws,
> Manholin', on my back—The cranks three inches off my nose.
> Romance ! Those first-class passengers they like it very well,
> Printed an' bound in little books ; but why don't poets tell ?
> I'm sick of all their quirks an' turns—the loves an' doves they dream.
> Lord, send a man like Robbie Burns to sing the Song o' Steam ! . . .
> Uplift am I ? When first in store the new-made beasties stood,
> Were Ye cast down that breathed the Word declarin' all things good ?
> Not so ! O' that world-liftin' joy no after-fall could vex,
> Ye've left a glimmer still to cheer the Man—the Arrtifex !
> *That* holds, in spite o' knock and scale, o' friction, waste an' slip,
> An' by that light—now, mark my word—we'll build the Perfect Ship.
> I'll never last to judge her lines or take her curve—not I.
> But I ha' lived an' I ha' worked. ' Be thanks to Thee, Most High ! ' "

This, then, is what we find in the modern world, and must take account of. We cannot keep machinery out, even if we would ; is it not our real task to humanize it ? An acute German observer thinks that in Britain we do not go the right way to work here : " we choose to ignore production by machinery ; we deny the possibility of any considerable artistic worth to anything not done by hand ; we refuse division of labour."[2] Is it not possible that these problems may finally be worked out better in America than with us ? Will not a new art grow there from a frankly practical stem ? For us, much

---

[1] *Seven Seas*, p. 43, " McAndrews's Hymn."
[2] *The Athenæum*, September 21, 1912, p. 317.

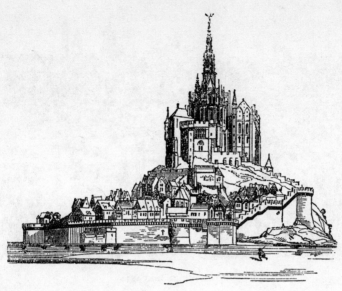

MONT ST.-MICHEL.

of the charm of the Gothic building lies in its natural and obvious adaptation to the practical requirements of its day. The typical picturesque in architecture is a crag-castle, or the crown of towers round a walled city ; the supreme example that comes first into our mind is the abbey-fortress of Mont St.-Michel, but the towers of Rothenburg on the Tauber are almost equally remarkable. Yet in all these cases it is the fact which shapes the art, not the art which controls the facts ; it is by taking full practical advantage of every ledge and every bit of cliff or slope that the masons have reared those walls and towers over which we linger with unfailing delight. So also, in our own day, if we are to make things as we want them to be, we must begin by taking things as they are.

It is necessary that a large number of modern buildings should be on an enormous scale. Quite apart from megalomania, which enters into this problem as into

ROTHENBURG (BAVARIA).

others, there is an undeniable need of vast structures. Therefore a new architecture of steel and concrete has grown up; and some men are growing up to the new conceptions implied by this enormous revolution. The late Sir Thomas Jackson, one of those who combined real scholarship with fine artistic taste and wide experience, wrote quite truly : " It is from the demands of utility that the best suggestions for advance in architecture have come in the past, and to them we must look in the future."[1] Here is robust sense and lofty optimism, in contrast to the reactionary writers whose theories amount in plain language to this, that we must substitute hand-work for machinery, and steadily keep the common people to one particular form of religion, in order that connoisseurs may enjoy the art which, under such hothouse treatment, the multitude will secrete for us. Thoughtful artists value such ideas at their true worth; and it would be difficult to express their feeling better than it has been recently expressed by one of them, in protest against the

[1] *Times Lit. Sup.*, November 22, 1923, p. 777.

exaggerations of a modern prophet. " Your criticism of modern industrial theory," he writes, " has been magnificent. It has never failed to be destructive. You have destroyed the gods which many a striving craftsman was tempted to worship. Surely that is sufficient for one man to accomplish. The creative ideas must come from the craftsmen themselves. If, fearless, they will go on producing the best they know, they will soon make a new economic system. And perhaps then they will enjoy your appreciation of their beautiful economy. But no craftsman cares a rap when you tell him that he ought not to work in the place he has selected as being the best suited for his work, or that people ought to buy ugly things merely because they are made in their own village. Show the craftsman that he is not as free as he thinks he is, and you will earn his eternal gratitude."

Let us apply this to America and the sky-scrapers and the necessary development of modern architecture. The craftsman here will not be free ; but free he never really was, at any time of really living and great art. The mass of craftsmen will be doing monotonous work, yet not necessary servile, any more than that of the medieval quarryman or the hard-hewer. A minority will be using their brains a good deal, in the adjustment of girders and the laying of concrete. A much smaller minority, again, will be doing higher supervision ; and one or two, at the top, will be real creators, real locomotives dragging the whole huge train along. What is there to be afraid of here, and why should not America succeed ?

The present volume has grown out of a course of American lectures, and is necessarily coloured by an experience, however brief and partial, of that country. It is strictly relevant, therefore, that I should repeat here, in this connexion, something of what was said there in a smaller company before whom even a semi-formal speech easily degenerated into a frank confession of the feelings of the moment, feelings called forth by that very visit and those experiences.

Men had told me that I should find the country and
the people widely different from my own. I was struck,
on the contrary, with the essential similarity of both, at
least as far west as Ohio, and as far south as Baltimore,
though this, of course, is not very far. And, everywhere,
I was haunted by those lines of George Herbert :—

> Religion stands on tip-toe in our land,
> Ready to pass to the American strand.

Here is a land that was colonized from ours at the very
time when Protestantism had justest causes of protest ;
a land where the basis of law is still English common-
law ; and in which, as in our own country, freedom has
broadened down from precedent to precedent in spite
of lapses and infidelities. Here are vast tracts, and a
teeming population, in which experiments once tried in
Europe can be tried again on a greater scale, and of
which we may also say in art what Samuel Daniel, three
centuries ago, said concerning the almost Roman univer-
sality which this new continent might give to the English
tongue :—

> " And who, in time, knows whither we may vent
>   The treasure of our tongue ?   To what strange shores
> This gain of our best glory shall be sent
>   To enrich unknowing nations with our stores ?
> What worlds in th' yet unformed Occident
>   May come refin'd with the accents that are ours ?
>
> Or who can tell for what great work in hand
>   The greatness of our style is now ordained ?
> What powers it shall bring in, what spirits command ?
>   What thoughts let out, what humours keep restrained ?
> What mischief it may powerfully withstand ?
>   And what fair ends may thereby be attained ? "

The fact that there is much materialism in a country
does not debar it from final excellence in art or in literature. I have already expressed my conviction that the
art of arts is the conduct of life ; of our own lives first,
and then of the lives which depend in any way upon us ;

and here, in spite of all that can be said on the other side, my belief is that America, as a whole, will stand comparison with any existing society, and must be ranked higher than some of the vaunted societies of the past. It is easy to exaggerate the moral and artistic disadvantages of money-getting. There is profound truth in Dr. Johnson's remark that a man is seldom more innocently employed than when he is making money, so long as we import no prejudices of our own into Johnson's plain words, but take them in their literal sense, and analyse straightforwardly the lesson they convey. In the light of sober experience, we have reason to distrust the persons or the peoples which boast that they are not money-getters. They are generally of that sort which makes a merit of carelessness and lack of foresight, and which tries to console itself for failure by despising the grapes that hang out of reach. Let a man first prove that he can make money, and then show his superiority to the mere money-getter by superior employment of that wealth and of his time. Some at least of the most artistic populations in history, for example, the Athenians and the Florentines, began as money-getters. On the other hand, medieval Rome was dead to healthy commerce and handiwork; it contained one of the most thriftless hand-to-mouth populations in Europe, and it produced practically no art beyond that of the few mosaic-workers who preyed on the great works of their ancestors. The popes had to import their artists from money-making districts. Britain, the nation of shopkeepers, has produced perhaps the finest body of poetry in the world. Art and literature, therefore, have nothing to fear in the long run from steel and steam and electricity; at the worst, we have only to wait till these things have found their equilibrium, as the Middle Ages had to ripen into that equilibrium of the thirteenth century.

But, however these things may be, one thing seems more and more certain; in our struggle for a better world, we cannot afford to neglect any good, whether in past history or in present society. And here there is no reason why the Protestant, in the truest and broadest sense of that word, should not join hands with Catholicity in its truest and broadest sense. Indeed, if we avoid artificial limitations of what ought to be sufficiently plain words, and artificial party exclusiveness, there is no real opposition between the two terms or the two ideas. *Protestant Catholic* is no more of a contradiction in terms than *Roman Catholic*, that time-honoured medieval phrase which is somewhat out of favour with the modern Roman Church. In proportion as a man clings to what seems Catholic (that is, universal) truth, he is bound to repudiate all that seems inconsistent with, or contradictory of, such universal truth. St. Paul and St. Peter were Protestants against idolatry ; St. Paul was a Protestant against the exclusive sectarian view of circumcision ; in far more recent times, some of the greatest of all Roman Catholics have protested most emphatically against religious abuses which were also among those most stoutly repudiated by our Reformers. And the one hope for the unity of Christendom—we may go farther, and say, for the harmony of all honest minds—lies in the acceptance of the widest field that is common to the largest number of thinking people. Indeed, I have recently heard something very like this, in public, from the lips of a prominent and earnest Roman Catholic ; corporate union seemed to him, at least for the present, outside of practical politics.

In all this discussion, we are in danger of losing sight of Walter Savage Landor's true order of things : " Nature I loved, and, next to nature, art." Or, as it has been put less formally in our own day : " Verses are made by fools like me, but only God can make a tree." The art of arts, let it be said again, is the art of life ; the accumulation and the harmony of all impressions and all human activities. In the Middle Ages, the men who corresponded to our present academics and critics, the people who wrote in Latin, were convinced, almost to a man, of the

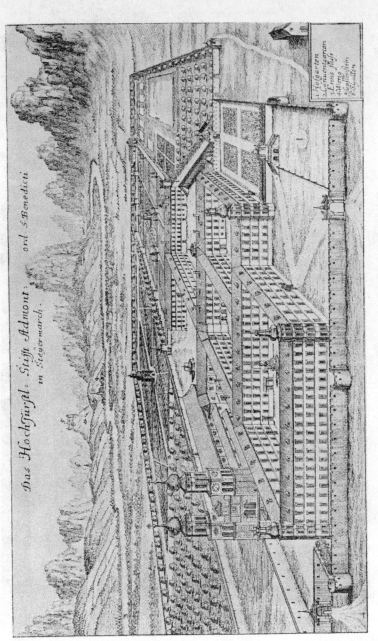

THE ABBEY OF ADMONT, STYRIA.

ST. MARGARET'S CHANCEL, LYNN.

hopeless and debasing inferiority of their own age to classical antiquity. They repeated this with an iteration that is wearisome to the modern reader. Meanwhile the medieval artisan, doing his own work as best he could, labouring in rivalry with his brethren, but also in harmony with them, and, as time went on and the work became greater and more complicated, labouring by the hundred in obedience to one single master— the artisan, I say, silently achieved what the scholastic philosopher knew to be impossible, and evolved something far greater, in its own way, than Greece or Rome had ever known. That was, in the main, the achievement of the common man, with whom it had been a toss-up whether he ploughed the land and made your bread, or stitched the leather and made your shoes, or made you these cathedrals. It was a product not of any part of the age alone, but of the whole age, of all humanity at that time ; it reflects the general tone of society. We see it even in the difference between the English and the French village churches. Here at home we have our elms, our meadow sloping down to the quiet brook, and the church most natural to those surroundings. There, in France, we have the sunburnt coteaux ; much of the field-work is in the more delicate task of vine-dressers, working among the fragile clear-cut tendrils and leaves, as distinguished from the simplicity or the old-world monotony of the plough and the cornfield.[1] Most French churches, therefore, ran higher

---

[1] Brutails notes how, at Bordeaux, when an artisan was settled enough to possess a house, there was generally a garden and a little bit of vineyard also (p. 44). Let us compare this with the fact that French flamboyant, even in its latest stages, never descended to the shallow platitudes of leaf-ornament which are too common in our Perpendicular. Even as far north as Amiens, "the culture of the vine and the vintage busied as many hands as the harvest" (A. de Calonne, in *Mém. Soc. Ant. Picardie.* 1880, p. 456). There may be some exaggeration here ; the facts quoted, though strong, are not conclusive ; also, there were far more vines in medieval England than now ; *e.g.*, the manor of Trumpington had a vineyard. But, on the whole, the contrast was very great then, as now.

than ours ; they were more costly, and the French sense
of sculpture is more delicate. But, whether here or there,
as we move among these buildings, we are the dreamers,
they the dream. Something as far-off and as tranquil as
sunset divides their world from that which we move in ;
their dusty work-day has worn onward into evening and
faded into afterglow ; the trees stand in arabesques
against the sky ; they have " a darkness that we feel is
green " ; it is a time of twilight and of dews. All that
was once fully-modelled is now cut out and stencilled in
flat filigree ; the tree is as beautiful as ever, yet with a
very different beauty. In a sense it is conventional and
imperfect now ; since we see it in only two dimensions ;
and our actual eyes will never grasp its full modelling,
for we are travellers passing on before to-morrow. Thus,
in the long-drawn vista of the centuries, we see medieval
life and art through a glass, darkly ; we may not see it
face to face, but it has none the less a reality of its own,
and, to many minds, a beauty beyond that of full
sunlight ; moreover, highest of all, a mystical beauty.
These common sights are capable of evoking the same
emotions as the porches of Chartres in the sunlight
under a June sky, or its aisles in the twilight, when the
jewelled windows stand out as the only realities in all that
solemn gloom.

In every religion there are things deeper even than
the sacraments ; and those deeper things are common to
all true faith. This is not to say that all creeds are the
same, but that some essential elements, at least, are
common to all. In every country and every age, mystics
have arrived at remarkably similar results ; and if either
art or nature stirs us to certain thoughts, it is commonly
because these existed already in germ, and because the
eye, in this case, brings that same stimulus which Sir
Thomas Browne ascribes in his own case to music. Side
by side with hours in English or Continental churches,
I cherish unforgettable memories of open-air Catholic
litanies, and open-air Revivalist hymns. Once on the

Upper Rhine, between Rheinfelden and Bâle, and once on its middle course, near the castle of Altenahr in the Ahrthal, and again in the Black Forest, I have had the same experience. A delicious deep summer twilight after a splendid day ; a wayside shrine ; and a group of work-folk, dark against the fading sky, led by one voice more earnest than the rest, almost painful in its tense devotion, chanting, alternately with the crowd, versicle and response of a vernacular litany. Again, earlier still, in the summer evenings of adolescence, driving to Westacre Church, under the shadow of the priory ruins. The road turns suddenly down to the ford under a little steepish slope of hill, waste and barren at the top, the neglected remnant of a common. There, up against the sky, in the slanting sunlight, was always a group of worshippers to whom the church seemed too narrow; we heard them singing " Hold the Fort ! " or " We shall meet on that beautiful shore." Here in Norfolk, as there in Rhineland, was an unmis-takable reality of tone ; rough or metallic voices which broke the cloying melody of those popular tunes ; all the softening and harmonizing effect of distance. Here, as there, the voices rose and fell upon the breeze and died away into the distance ; the hour and the open air and the woodland scenery purged them of all commonplace everyday associations ; they went up like incense ; and when, an hour later, we ourselves were singing our last hymn in Westacre Church, and the sun had stolen through the northern windows, to fall upon the white angel-tomb in the chancel, then in our hearts we all bore that other open-air music also. For nobody has the monopoly either of religion or of religious art ; nor need we to fear that either the one or the other is dead. We may get now, as men got in the past, as much of either as we are willing to pay the just price for ; Baron von Hügel, we are told, always insisted on that word *cost* in religion. In the material sense, we may get religion on Isaiah's terms, without money and without price ; but, in the spiritual sense, every man in every age must work out his own salvation.

And that is why I am steeled against the attempt to put a sectarian ring-fence round Gothic art, with a sectarian turnstile for admittance. The attempt is as absurd in practice as it is in history ; for nature laughs at these artificial obstacles. For one man who persuades himself that, because he loves Chartres, therefore he must accept the theological formulæ of the men who built it, there will always be many others who love its self, and perhaps love it more deeply, without the need of such illusion. It is the case of Lovelace's " I could not love thee, dear, so much, loved I not honour more " ; it is the case of William Morris, of whom it might be said as truly as of Matthew Arnold that " he was never a Romantic in the bad sense of the word— namely, an artist who will submit to the lie of the soul for the purposes of his art." And it is the same, in different degrees, with thousands more who reverence these buildings, who reverence their builders and all truth in the religion with which these men are connected, yet who thank God daily that they were born in an age in which men are free to be Protestants, or Catholics, or both, or neither. Among those thousands I have the right to count myself. It was Gothic art, sixty years ago, that first kindled in me the love of the Middle Ages. Afternoon service at St. Margaret's, Lynn, where even children might sit in the choir-stalls, and we walked to our places (*horresco referens !*) over two of the most beautiful monumental brasses in the world, and sat there under some of the fairest thirteenth century stonework and fourteenth century wood-carving in England, is an unforgettable recollection. In Westminster Abbey or one of our cathedrals, or sometimes at Mass in France, there is a glow of feeling and a rush of thoughts which warms and illuminates like sunshine. We are wrong if we do not welcome these things ; but we are wrong also if we identify them too closely with the Christian religion.

They may help us to worship God in spirit and in truth ; but, on the other hand, they may stand between us and God. They were not there in the earliest days ; the best of the primitive Christians did without them.[1] If we care deeply for these things which St. Bernard and St. Francis neglected, it may possibly be because we have higher artistic sensibilities than they, but it certainly is not because we are more religious. The indiscriminate identification of art and a particular religion is no real compliment to either.

And, in one very real sense, it would seem positively unchristian ; it would seem to shut us off from Christian hope. For, if we take even the most eloquent of these lamentations over the past, they do but recall the dignified melancholy of Lucretius—*mortalem vitam mors immortalis ademit*—our mortal art has been swallowed up in immortal death. But this, put into Bible words, is tantamount to a proclamation that the gates of hell have prevailed against medieval art ; and to this the Bible-Christian will answer with St. Paul : " God forbid. . . . Death is swallowed up in victory ! " After Attila's pillage, St. Jerome cried in despair, " When Rome falls, what is left standing ? " But it was then that St. Augustine sat down to write his *City of God*. That brave and inspiring book has two abiding lessons for all time. First, that we have no need to regret the passing of a former civilization, so long as we ourselves have faith and courage enough to save what treasure there is to be saved from among the ruins.

[1] This remains true, even if we take the Catacomb pictures of Rome at the earliest date assigned to them. In perhaps the majority of cases, these are simply pagan motives adopted by the Christians ; again, they do not represent the official teaching of the Church at that time. It is incredible that all the early apologists should have spoken of image-worship as non-existent among Christians, if this repudiation had not been true in fact. For, it must be remembered, they had every temptation to exaggerate in the other direction ; the pagan accusations of atheism could have been refuted in a single sentence if they had been able to say " we do in fact secretly paint Christ and the Virgin Mary and the saints, and say our prayers before them."

And, secondly, that this change should bring us not despair but hope ; the things which have perished beyond recall are those which were doomed to perish ; true, the New Jerusalem must be built with the sword in one hand and the trowel in the other ; yet for those who build in the spirit, and on a spiritual foundation, there can be no final failure. In the material sense, Rome is fallen ; ancient Rome is indeed fallen ; but " there remaineth a Sabbath-rest for the people of God." [1]

[1] Augustine, *De Civ. Dei*, bk. xxii, c. 30.

APPENDIX 25.—(CHAP. XVI. p. 327)

SIR RICHARD JEBB'S PAMPHLET

HAS ART THRIVEN BEST IN AN AGE OF FAITH ? A paper read before members of the Glasgow Art Club, March 25, 1889. (Glasgow, Veir and Richardson, 1889.)

SIR RICHARD begins with a clear definition : " I am using the phrase, ' an Age of Faith,' in the special sense in which it has sometimes been employed—viz., to denote an age in which the artist, and those for whose delight he works, are alike possessed by an untroubled faith in some form of religious doctrine ; and when the artist, in treating of religious themes, is at once expressing and satisfying a religious enthusiasm." He first considers the subject generally, and confesses that, at first sight, history might seem to answer *Yes* (p. 6). " The development of Greek sculpture and of Italian painting lends some apparent force to the contention that Art has never been so excellent as when it has been inspired by religion ; it was the glow of a devout faith that lifted the imagination of Greek sculptor and Italian painter into a region of beauty higher than they could have reached by any weaker aid." But he concludes that this answer, however plausible at first sight, is not in accordance with the real facts. First, he takes the case of Greece (p. 9) : " The period during which Pheidias flourished was from 450 to 432 B.C. At that time the popular religion was still, indeed, in full external vigour ; there was no decadence in the ritual of the temples, the sacrifices, and the festivals. But, by the side of the popular religion, there was also an esoteric religion, that of men who could no longer believe in the Homeric gods or the temple myths, but who cherished a more simple faith in a divine government of the world. And there were also some who had cut adrift from all religious belief. Pheidias was the friend of Pericles ; the society in which he lived was doubtless that of the keenest intellects of his day. Glorious

as were the forms which he gave to the popular gods, it is most
improbable that the spirit in which he worked was that of one
who regarded them with the devout faith of the simpler folk ;
rather, it must have been purely the spirit of the artist and the
poet—in imaginative sympathy with a popular belief which
was not his own." And again (p. 11) : the artistic productions
of earlier ages in Greece are rude and marked by a rigid adherence
to traditional types. "They belonged to an age of simple
dogmatic faith. In the age of Pheidias there were many men
who, like the Ionian Herodotus or the Athenian Nicias, stood
firmly on the ancient ways ; there was also a believing multitude ;
but it was not, in respect to most of the finer minds, an age
of faith." So, again, with Italy in the fifteenth century : " The
influence of the Renaissance had, as a matter of fact, been to
weaken the hold of doctrinal Catholicism on the cultivated
classes. But this did not directly affect Art. The point which
I desire to mark is this : that the period at which Italian
painting was best was not that at which the hold of religious
faith on artists was strongest ; and that the heightened excellence
of Art was due to a cause wholly independent of religion, just
as little was the decadence of Italian painting towards the end
of the sixteenth century connected in any way with a decline
of religious faith " (p. 15). " If, then, we ask what is the
teaching of history on this point, the answer must be as follows :
Religion has indeed supplied Art with its loftiest themes, and
has received in tribute some of Art's greatest achievements ;
but the artistical result has owed its excellence to an artistic,
and not to a religious motive. When Raphael painted a
Madonna, the very nature of the subject constrained him to
present human beauty in the highest and purest form that he
could conceive. But, as an artist, he would do this equally,
whether he was or was not in mental accord with the doctrinal
teaching of his church. If to any this seem a truism, I would
only venture to observe that it has not always, and to all men,
seemed a truism. We have sometimes heard language held by
critics of repute which implied that for us, in this age and in this
country, the supreme inspiration of Art had for ever passed
away, along with that attitude towards Catholicism which
prevailed in medieval Europe." And, finally, on the wider
question of art's relation to morality and religion, he concludes
(p. 21) : " Art, whether consciously or unconsciously, must
always be producing some moral effect on those who view its

works. And Art is doing moral good in the way proper to it as Art, when, whatever its form or subject, it brings the beholder's mind into a genuine relation with natural beauty—in other words, whenever it enables the beholder to see the beauty of the created universe, animate or inanimate, with a new vividness of perception. And to do that is to serve Religion in the largest and truest sense of the word, in a sense which would have been acknowledged equally by John Knox and by St. Francis; for, when Art is most herself, then it is that she gives visible form to the precept of that sublime hymn—that utterance in which the Catholic Church of medieval Christendom is so wholly at one with our own age, in every Christian communion—

'O all ye works of the Lord, bless ye the Lord;
praise Him and magnify Him for ever.'"

APPENDIX 26.—(CHAP. XVI, p. 331)

ST. BERNARD AND PETER THE PRECENTOR

(a) St. Bernard. *Letter to Abbot William of St.-Thierry.*

" I SAY naught of the vast height of your [Cluniac] churches, their immoderate length, their superfluous breadth, the costly polishings, the curious carvings and paintings which attract the worshipper's gaze and hinder his attention, and seem to me in some sort a revival of the Ancient Jewish rites. Let this pass, however : say that this is done for God's honour. But I, as a monk, ask of my brother monks . . . 'tell me, ye poor (if, indeed, ye be poor), what doeth this gold in your sanctuary ? ' And indeed the bishops have an excuse which monks have not ; for we know that they, being debtors both to the wise and the unwise, and unable to excite the devotion of carnal folk by spiritual things, do so by bodily adornments. But we [monks] who have now come forth from the people ; we who have left all the precious and beautiful things of the world for Christ's sake ; who have counted but dung, that we may win Christ, all things fair to see or soothing to hear, sweet to smell, delightful to taste, or pleasant to touch—in a word, all bodily delights— whose devotion, pray, do we monks intend to excite by these things ? What profit, I say, do we expect therefrom ? The admiration of fools, or the oblations of the simple ? Or, since we are scattered among the nations, have we perchance learnt their works and do we yet serve their graven images ? To speak plainly, doth the root of all this lie in covetousness, which is idolatry ; and do we seek not [spiritual] profit, but a gift ? If thou askest : ' How ? ' I answer, ' In a strange fashion.' For money is thus artfully scattered in order that it may multiply ; it is expended that it may give increase, and prodigality giveth birth to plenty ; for at the very sight of these costly yet marvel- lous vanities men are more kindled to offer gifts than to pray. Thus wealth is drawn up by ropes of wealth, thus money bringeth money ; for I know not how it is that, wheresoever more abundant wealth is seen, there do men offer more freely. Their eyes are feasted with relics cased in gold, and their purse-strings are loosed. They are shown a most comely image of some saint, whom they think all the more saintly that he is the more gaudily painted. Men run to kiss him, and are invited to give ; there is more admiration for his comeliness than veneration for his sanctity. . . . The church is resplendent in her walls, beggarly in her poor ; she clothes her stones in gold, and leaves her sons naked ; the rich man's eye is fed at the expense of the indigent. The curious find their delight here, yet the needy find no relief. Do we not revere at least the images of the Saints, which swarm even in the inlaid pavement whereon we tread ? Men spit oftentimes in an Angel's face; [this is so shocking to the latest orthodox biographer of the Saint, that he takes the liberty of omitting it (*Life of St. Bernard*, by A. J. Luddy, *O. Cist*, p. 109). Otherwise, however, Fr. Luddy makes no attempt to minimize the bearing and the effect of this letter.] Often, again, the countenance of some Saint is ground under the heel of a passer-by. And if he spare not these sacred images, why not even the fair colours ? Why dost thou make that so fair which will soon be made so foul ? Why lavish bright hues upon that which must needs be trodden under foot ? What avail these comely forms in places where they are defiled with customary dust ? And, lastly, what are such things as these to you poor men, you monks, you spiritual folk ? Unless perchance here also ye may answer the poet's question in the words of the Psalmist : ' Lord, I have loved the habitation of Thy house, and the place where Thine honour dwelleth.' I grant it, then, let us suffer even this to be done in the church ; for, though it be harmful to vain and covetous folk, yet not so to the simple and devout. But in the cloister, under the eyes of the Brethren who read there, what profit is there in those ridiculous monsters, in that marvellous and deformed comeliness, that comely deformity ? To what purpose are those unclean apes, those fierce lions, those monstrous centaurs, those half-men, those striped tigers, those fighting knights, those hunters winding their horns ? Many bodies are there seen under one head, or again, many heads to a single body. Here is a four-footed beast with a serpent's tail; there, a fish with a beast's head. Here again, the forepart of a horse trails half a goat behind it, or a horned beast bears the hind quarters of a horse. In short, so many and so marvellous are the varieties of divers shapes on every hand, that we are more tempted to read in the marble than in our books, and to spend the whole day in wondering at these things rather than in meditating the law of God. For God's sake, if men are not ashamed of these follies, why at least do they not shrink from the expense ? "

(*b*) Petrus Cantor. (*Verbum Abbreviatum*, c. 86.) Nearly two generations later than St. Bernard.

" Christians ought rather to exhort each other, saying : ' We have not here a lasting city, but we seek one that is to come . . . ' As one prelate said to another, ' What meaneth this loftiness of your buildings ? Wherefore have ye towers and bulwarks withal ? Thou shalt not thereby be better defended against the Devil, but all the nearer to him.' Moreover, this lust of building is testified by the palaces of princes, reared from the tears and the money wrung from the poor. But monastic or ecclesiastical edifices are raised from the usury and breed of barren metal among covetous men, from the lying deceits and deceitful lies of hireling preachers ; and what-soever is built from ill-gotten gains is in much peril of ruin ; for, as Ovid saith, ' A sordid prey hath no good issue.' For example, St. Bernard wept to see the shepherds' huts thatched with straw, like unto the first huts of the Cistercians, who were then beginning to live in palaces of stone, set with all the stars of heaven. But oftentimes to the Religious themselves, as to other men, their own offence becomes an instrument to punish them for this disease of building ; for the construction of comely and ample houses is an invitation to proud guests. Even the granges of the monks are oftentimes castellated in self-defence."

APPENDIX 27.—(Chap. XVII, p. 346)

ARCHITECTURAL FINANCE

(*a*) It is instructive to summarize the different sources of revenue for the fabric fund at Autun Cathedral in 1294, as analysed by Quicherat (*Mélanges*, vol. II, pp. 185 ff).

These are (1) Tax on the Chapter. Receipts £160 5*s*.; arrears £68 17*s*. (2) From vacant benefices in diocese, which Pope allows to be taxed, £12 10*s*. (3) Indulgences, £24 18*s*. 4*d*. (4) Subscriptions (from clergy ?) at Pentecostal synod, £12 11*s*. 7*d*. (5) Casual receipts, including several legacies, all from peasants except one *magister*, a clerk, £34 19*s*. 5*d*. (Includes also almsboxes in different churches.) (6) Alms-boxes in other churches, regularly kept for this work; also shares of indulgences, £10 17*s*. 2*d*. (7) Additional Chapter tax, £42 13*s*. 3*d*.

Among the expenses is an item of £1 10*s*. for the scribes copying the letters of indulgence.

(*b*) Again, Quicherat analyses the Troyes Cathedral fabric fund receipts from 1373 to 1380 (ibid., p. 194). The sources are (1) Entrance fee for newly-elected canons (£13 6*s*. 8*d*. each). (2) Endowments for the fabric fund. (3) Fees charged to pilgrims for showing the relics, or touching their linen with the relics. (4) Freewill offerings before the relics. (5) Contents of boxes placed in all churches of diocese. (6) Ditto of boxes in churches of Troyes. (7) From collectors who carried relics about. This job was now farmed out to a layman, on a three years' lease, for £20 a year. (8) Money paid for anniversary Masses and services for the dead. (9) Payments in corn for the same anniversaries, etc. (10) Subscriptions from diocesan Chapters. (11) Hiring out of palls for funerals. (12) Legacies of money, clothes, etc. (13) Offerings at the Mass of the Holy Ghost every Monday. (14) From three gilds which had their services in the cathedral. (15) Extraordinary receipts, from certain New Year's Masses, fines for trespasses on church lands, etc. (16) Friars' sermons in aid of the fabric. For instance, the Lector of the

Franciscans preached in 1372, and they gave him bread and
wine to cost of 6s. 10d. Later on in the same year a Dominican
preached for them. (17) About 1382, the Cathedral obtained
bulls of indulgences from Pope Clement, for which they laid
out £6. (18) In 1385 the Bishop laid the first stone of the
pulpitum and paid £5 ; a canon gave 5s. for laying the second
stone ; another £2 for a vault for his coffin under the pulpitum.

(c) Quicherat analyses similarly the accounts of St.-Ouen at
Rouen, under nine different heads (ibid., p. 222 ; A.D. 1321).

(d) When Chapter XVII was already printed, Miss K. Wood-
Legh drew my attention to four entries in the *Calendars of Papal
Letters*, which showed how parish endowments were appropriated
—and, as most of us would feel, unfairly appropriated—to the
fabric of some church of which, in some cases, parishioners can
never have heard. In 1306 the brethren of Sempringham obtained
papal licence thus to swallow up the parish revenues of Thur-
stanton and Norton Disny " to rebuild their monastery." In
1320 the canons of Hereford, impoverished for the moment by
their building expenses and by what they had paid to the papal
court for the canonization of their bishop, St. Thomas de Cantilupe,
were allowed to appropriate Scenigfeld. In 1343, St. Peter's at
Northampton, with two dependent chapelries, was appropriated
to the hospital of St. Katharine by the Tower, which " has begun
to build a fair church." In 1363, St. Thomas of Salisbury was
appropriated to the Cathedral repairs for six years. (*C.P.L.*,
I, p. 462 ; II, pp. 14, 196 ; III, p. 88 ; IV, p. 89.)

By way of comparison, readers may be interested to see what
has been done by different Masters and Fellows of one of the
smaller Cambridge Colleges (St. Catharine's) for the building and
the educational endowment of their own house. It will be seen
that they do not suffer by comparison with the Middle Ages.
HUGH GARNETT, Fellow of the College, besides other gifts, gave
in 1526 his lands, messuages, and moveable goods. EDMUND
HOUND, Master, left in 1577 a legacy of £100. THOMAS BUCK,
Fellow of the College, gave much help towards the completion,
in the year 1630, of the building thence called after his own name.
JOHN EACHARD, Master, devoted his private fortune to the
rebuilding of the College. By his own gifts and by the gifts
of others he provided over £10,000 for the new buildings. JOHN
SLADER and DANIEL MILLS, Fellows of the College, gave towards
the rebuilding the former £200, the latter £160. PETER FISHER,
JAMES CALAMY, OFSPRING BLACKHALL, Bishop of Exeter, and

JOHN JEFFERY, Archdeacon of Norwich, all formerly Fellows of the College, gave much help towards the new buildings; as did also all the Fellows of the College then existing, by resigning much of the profits of their Fellowships. SIR WILLIAM DAWES, Baronet, Master of the House and Archbishop of York, gave three years' profits of the Mastership towards building the Chapel. He gave further, in the year 1714, £100 to release an annuity payable by the College, and made annual payments up to the time of his death towards other annuities. JOHN ADDENBROOKE, M.D., formerly Fellow of the College, the Founder of Addenbrooke's Hospital in this town, left a legacy of £110. JOHN LENG, Bishop of Norwich, formerly Fellow of the College, left by will £20, having before benefited the College by the resignation of much of the profits of his Fellowship. Dr. CROSS and Dr. HUBBARD, Masters, gave, the former a tenement and gardens adjoining the College, the latter a legacy of £40. THOMAS SHERLOCK, Master and then Bishop of London, gave lands and tenements to increase the stipend of the Master's Sizar and to found a Librarians' Scholarship. He gave also his library of books and £620 towards fitting up the Library. JOSEPH PROCTOR, Master, gave during his lifetime £1,000 and also purchased land to increase the revenues of the Mastership. He died intestate, but his nephew and heir-at-law, FRANCIS PROCTOR, Fellow of the College, made over the property which Dr. PROCTOR had intended to bequeath. CHARLES WILLIAM BURRELL, Fellow of the College, gave certain lands during his lifetime to increase the dividends of the Fellows, and also gave £1,000 in cash. At his death in 1843 he left to the College £8,000, the greater part of his private property. EDMUND YORKE, for fifty-three years Fellow of the College, at his death in 1873 left £4,000 for the educational purposes of the College. THOMAS WORTLEY DRURY, Bishop of Ripon, Master, founded an Exhibition for students desiring Holy Orders and did much for the adornment of the Chapel.

APPENDIX 28.—(Chap. XVII, p. 361)

ETON INDULGENCES

(Sir H. Maxwell Lyte. *Hist. of Eton College*, 1911, p. 9.)

'HIS [Henry VI's] envoys in Italy were instructed to apply for Papal Indulgences, which would attract strangers to Eton, and make its name famous throughout England. They succeeded in obtaining a bull granting to all penitents who should thenceforth visit the Collegiate Church of Eton at the feast of the Assumption in August, Indulgences equal to those which could be obtained on the 1st of that month at the church of St. Peter ad Vincula at Rome. All those who wished to partake of these privileges were ordered to contribute towards the maintenance of the College, and expected to offer prayers for the Founder. A year, however, had not quite elapsed from the date of this bull, before Eugenius the Fourth was induced to enlarge its provisions, by making the Indulgence plenary instead of partial, although limited to the lifetime of Henry the Sixth. Nevertheless, he warily introduced a clause enacting that three-quarters of the offerings of the penitents should be devoted towards the defence of Christendom against the Turks, an object in which he naturally felt more interest than he could feel in the prosperity of a new college in a distant land. The Bishop of Bath, the Chancellor of England, was entrusted with only one key of the alms-box at Eton, the other being committed to the Pope's collector. Chester and Caunton must have represented that these changes did not effect all that was desired by their royal master, for another bull was issued in favour of Eton a few weeks later. The Provost was thereby authorized to hear the confessions of all members of the College, either personally or by deputy, and, if desirable, to release them from excommunications, suspensions and interdicts, and even to absolve them once in cases specially reserved for the consideration of the Holy See. Inasmuch as the penances were in some cases

to be continued by the heirs of deceased penitents, it is evident
that they must have ordinarily consisted of monetary payments.
The Pope, however, tried to guard against persons committing
deliberate sin in the expectation of an easy absolution, by making
certain fasts a certain part of the penance. Soon after the receipt
of the Bulls of Indulgence, Archbishop Chicheley wrote to the
Bishop of Exeter, ordering him to publish them in his diocese,
and describing them as more ample than any hitherto issued
by any Pope. The King, too, had his tents repaired ' on account
of the Indulgence to be had,' at his College of Eton, perhaps
with a view to providing shelter to visitors. It would appear
that the payment made to the Roman Court ' for one Indulgence '
amounted to more than £158. The acceptance or publication
of papal bulls was strictly illegal in England at this period under
the Statute of Provisors, and offenders were liable to suffer
forfeiture of their property, and indefinite imprisonment of
their persons. Henry the Sixth therefore took care to provide
against such a contingency in the case of the members of his new
College, by issuing to them a pardon for all bulls already received,
and a general licence to receive others in future. In May 1443,
a third agent was despatched to Italy, in the person of Dr.
Vincent Clement, a papal chaplain, for whom Henry the Sixth
had, with some difficulty, obtained a degree at the University
of Oxford."

APPENDIX 29.—(CHAP. XVIII, p. 374)

DIVES AND PAUPER ON IDOLATRY

THE statement in my text is sufficiently startling to need a documentary voucher here, especially as the incident is typical of the treatment of this and similar subjects in books which are widely read.

Cardinal Gasquet, in a volume called *Monastic Life in the Middle Ages* (Bell and Sons, 1922), reprinted an earlier essay on " How our Fathers were taught." He there undertakes to disprove the idea that the Reformers had real religious justification for their destruction of images and whitewashing of walls ; and he quotes largely from the dialogue of *Dives and Pauper*, which was probably written by a Franciscan friar about A.D. 1400, and which is certainly one of our best authorities for this and similar subjects. But this is a very rare book ; and, since the Cardinal nowhere gives a single reference to section or chapter which might help the reader to check his quotations, any unfortunate student who wished to follow the matter up might waste many hours in the search. Under cover of this silence, the Cardinal treats *Dives and Pauper* by a method which can be exposed only by printing here nearly a page from his book (p. 75). He there writes : " One of the boasted reforms of the early English Protestants was that they had put a stop to the adoration which was paid to the cross and in particular had forbidden the retention in the service of Good Friday of any semblance of the old practice of honouring it by what was known as ' creeping ' to it ; that is approaching it with bended knee. It was claimed that by allowing this customary reverence, the Church had given occasion for the growth of serious superstition among the common people, amounting in reality to practical idolatry. In view of this it is interesting to see how Pauper deals with this question :—

 ' [On Good Friday],' says Dives, ' especially in Holy Church, men creep to the cross and worship the cross.—That is so [replies the teacher], but not in the way that thou meanest. The cross that we creep to and worship so highly at that time is Christ Himself, who died on the cross on that day and for our sake ... But He is that cross, as all doctors say, to whom we pray and say "*Ave crux spes unica*—Hail thou cross, our only hope."—But [rejoins Dives] on Palm Sunday, at the procession, the priest draweth up the veil before the Rood and falleth down to the ground with all the people, saying thrice thus: "*Ave Rex noster*—Hail, be Thou our King!" In this he worships the image as king!—Pauper: Absit! God forbid! He speaks not to the image that the carpenter hath made and the painter painted, unless the priest be a fool, for the stock and stone was never king. He speaketh to Him that died on the cross for us all—to Him that is King of all things ... For this reason are crosses placed by the wayside, to remind folk to think of Him who died on the cross, and worship Him above all things. And for this same reason is the cross borne before a procession, that all who follow after it or meet it should worship Him who died upon a cross as their King, their Head, their Lord, and their Leader to heaven.' "

So far writes and quotes Cardinal Gasquet; and certainly, to any incautious reader who fails to weigh these words from *Dives and Pauper* again and again, and to note their inconclusiveness, they do give superficial colour to his contention that there was no danger of idolatry, and that the Reformers' iconoclasm had no religious justification. But when we look at the original, and realize the significance of the omission which is represented by those three unemphatic dots, we find that a whole column has been left out, so that the passage thus suppressed is actually longer than the passages which Cardinal Gasquet has thought fit to print. And, stranger still, that omitted column flatly negatives the apology which the Cardinal has painfully constructed from those mutilated remnants which he has put before his readers! For, in that column, the good friar expresses his regret that some of the Church services do in fact lend themselves to most regrettable misunderstandings as to worship of the cross. The official language, he writes, " blindeth much folk in their redynge.[1] For they mean that all the prayers that Holy Church maketh to the Cross, that she maketh them to the tree that Christ died on, or else to the cross in the church, as in that anthem, *O crux splendidior*. And so for lewdness they be deceived, and worship

---

[1] I.e. *interpretation*. The elementary medieval dictionary called *Promptorium Parvulorum* gives " Redynge=*Interpretacio*." *Mean*, of course, is used for *think* in the English of that date. So *tree* is commonly used for *wood*, and *lewd* for *illiterate*.

creatures as God Himself " (Com. I, ch. 4, ed. Berthelet f. 15b).
Moreover, the author recognizes the seriousness of such mistaken devotions ; for he writes : " Therefore they who make
their prayers and their praises before images and say their
Pater noster and their *Ave Maria* and other prayers and praises
commonly used by Holy Church, or any other such, if they do it
to the image and speak to the image they do open idolatry. Also
they are not excused even if they understand not what they say,
for their lights and their other wits, and their inner wit also,
showeth well that there ought that no such prayer, praise, or
worship should be offered to such images, for they can neither
hear them, nor see them, nor help them in their needs." This
passage Cardinal Gasquet quotes on p. 77 in support of his
contention that there was no serious danger of idolatry ; whereas,
when we restore that crucial column which he has taken the
liberty of suppressing, this farther quotation adds emphasis to
the already acknowledged danger.

APPENDIX 30.—(Chap. XX, p. 407)

ART AND PURITANISM

I HAVE dealt more fully with this subject in *From St. Francis to Dante*, and in vol. I of *Five Centuries of Religion* (see indexes under *Puritanism*). I had not then the advantage of reading Mr. Joseph Crouch's *Puritanism and Art* (Cassell, 1910), a book which justifies its sub-title : *An Enquiry into a Popular Fallacy*. The author is not a medievalist, but his occasional inaccuracies in this field supply an indirect testimonial to his honest attempt to see both sides ; they are quite as often, and perhaps oftener, " to his own hurt " than not. He shows how far even pre-Reformation art had lost touch with the people (p. 79), and how the objections of the early Reformers rested not on aesthetic indifference, but on serious doctrinal differences (chapter V, esp. pp. 106–7, 126–8). He emphasizes the vandalism of Laud, who regarded art, as the Puritans did, rather from the theological than the aesthetic point of view (p. 158) ; he shows how Mary I, like her doctrinal antagonists, regarded the theatre more from the political and social than from the artistic point of view (272 ; cf. 281) ; how little the post-Reformation Roman Church has done for the best art (301) ; and, on the other hand, how much has been done for religious art of their own accord by great Protestants like Dürer (305 ff.), Rembrandt (320 ff.), and the English landscapists, of whom so many came from the same district as Cromwell's Ironsides (336 ff.). No student can neglect this book who really wishes to see both sides of the question.

APPENDIX 31.—(CHAP. XX, p. 418)

ARCHITECTURE AND NATURAL SCENERY

(a) Ruskin, *Seven Lamps*, Bk. III, §§ 23, 24.

" THE relative majesty of buildings depends more on the weight and vigour of their masses than on any other attribute of their design ; mass of everything, of bulk, of light, of darkness, of colour, not mere sum of any of these, but breadth of them ; not broken light, nor scattered darkness, nor divided weight, but solid stone, broad sunshine, starless shade. . . . It matters not how clumsy, how common the means are, that get weight and shadow—sloping roof, jutting porch, projecting balcony, hollow niche, mossy gargoyle, frowning parapet ; get but gloom and simplicity, and all good things will follow in their place and time ; do but design with the owl's eyes first, and you will gain the falcon's afterwards. . . . We have other sources of power, in the imagery of our iron coasts and azure hills ; of power more pure nor less serene than that of the hermit spirit which once lighted with white lines of cloisters the glades of the Alpine pine, and raised into ordered spires the wild rocks of the Norman sea ; which gave to the temple gate the depth and darkness of Elijah's Horeb cave ; and lifted, out of the populous city, grey cliffs of lonely stone, into the midst of sailing birds and silent air."

(b) Der Jüngere Titurel. (Sulpiz Boisserée, *Ueber die Beschreibung des Tempels u.s.w.*, 1835 ; cf. Blanca Röthlisberger, *Die Architektur des Graltempels u.s.w.*, Bern, 1917.)

This poem, written by Albrecht von Scharffenberg in about 1270, is a continuation of Wolfram von Eschenbach's unfinished *Parsifal*. Early in the poem, Albrecht describes how King Titurel built a temple for the Holy Grail. The Grail had here the talismanic power of fulfilling every wish of its possessor with regard to the temple ; thus the King dreamed his building into actuality, and we have a perfect edifice without a single

human workman. This conception gives full licence to the poet ;
he may give the freest possible rein to his imagination ; and,
from one point of view, this adds special significance to his
elaborate picture of the Graal-Temple.

The German poet, like Chaucer, shows frequent disregard of
the actual artistic traditions of his own day ; and it is noteworthy that so many of his imaginations turn towards the direct
imitation of nature. This temple of the Holy Grail, resembling
in general construction a late Romanesque church, is designed
in many details to transport us straight to the forest or the sea-
shore. The matters upon which dogmatic symbolism would
lay most stress are passed over rapidly. There are angels, and
apostles, and the Crucifix, and the Virgin, and the Last Judgment ; the figures are so impressive that " rude folk would
think them alive " ; but all this is briefly told (strophes 7, 8, 100
in Boisserée). The portals, again, are set with precious stones,
and golden letters rehearsing the occult virtues of each stone ;
but this is by no means peculiar to Christianity (94). Outside,
were two long friezes of sculpture, that showed fighting Templar
Knights and dwarves and sea-monsters interwoven with vines
(49, 50) ; this work moves the poet to admiration : " I tell
you truly, if my neighbour would scan that marvellous carving
from end to end, he might well stand there until his housewife
had finished her dinner." But here, again, is nothing which
differs, artistically, from what might have been carved on a
Walhalla. The poet's highest efforts are spent upon the choir
arcade and the organ at the west end of the temple. In the choir,
above the stalls and the carved screens of precious wood, rise
the great arches on pillars of bronze ; from each capital there
grows a vine, which climbs to the crown of the arch and thence
descends, intertwining with its sister-vine from the neighbouring
pillar ; both together " hung down a good fathom and a half
over the stalls. Beneath, it was set with marvellous flowers,
with roses sprouting white on trees and twigs ; white lilies,
again, with their green leaves and stems ; there could the earnest
gazer see the counterfeit colours of all precious flowers, the blossom
of every herb that grows, of all high and noble herbs ; of all
such could a man see some counterfeit trembling there in beauty,
with hue and form that matched them well, stem and leaf and
flower and tendril, and all in a thicket of gold. The vines were
of solid gold, yet green-enamelled, for counterfeiting of the vine
and for gladdening of men's eyes, and for the shade that it gave

from many a wondrous gleam, so that all the walls of this choir were almost draped in emerald. The branches hung so thick that, when any breeze stirred, then men heard them tinkle gently in sweet harmony, even as though a thousand falcons should hover in a flock, with all their golden bells ringing together. Over these vines hung many a cloud of angels, as though they were fresh from Paradise ; and when the vine branches began their melody, then the angels moved like living souls."

So, again, with the organ-loft at the west end (97–100). There was wrought "a tree of red, red gold, with leaf and branch and twig, whereon there sat, as had been devised, a throng of fowls on every hand, of the best that men praise for their sweetest strains ; and, when the organ-bellows blew, then sang each after his own song. One sang high and another low, even as the keys moved them ; the wind, by cunning work, rustled hither and thither in the tree ; well knew the organ-master which of the fowls he would impel ; well knew he the key that moved each to sing. Four angels stood firm on the top of the topmost branches, each with a golden horn in hand ; mighty was the blast they blew, and with their other hand they beckoned, as who should cry, ' Awake, up, dead men all ! ' There stood the Last Doom, not painted, but cast [in bronze] ; clear was the warning that came from the rueful faces of the sinners, so that the sour should go ever with the sweet, and man, in his hours of joy, should bethink him of that day of mourning."

Most original of all, perhaps, is the pavement of this Grail-Temple (101–103). The building was founded on a rock of onyx ; and " here below on this onyx were graven and carved fishes and figures of every sort of sea-monster, each in his proper form ; they moved even as though they were wild creatures. For pipes from without ran in all round, and the pavement was of crystal clear, under which they flickered in these gusts even as though they lived in the waves ; the bellows that breathed this life into them were moved by far-off windmills. Thus did the pavement delight men's eyes and show as a sea with wallowing waves, yet covered all with ice, so clear that there-through men saw a whole world of fishes and beasts and monsters of the deep, with restless stress and storm."

We have, in this last episode, a living commentary on many of Villard's problems that might otherwise seem trivial to us. In their pleasant hours of evening speculation over the wine-pot or on the tavern bench, these medieval workmen threw out many hints which might bear indirectly, if not quite directly, most excellent fruit. This living sea under the crystal floor was indeed possible only in the romance of Titurel, where the Grail itself has the virtues of Aladdin's lamp, and where Albrecht can say here, as the Bible tells us of Solomon's temple, that all these marvels were wrought without sound of axe and hammer. But in the actual mason's or carpenter's shop, where axe and hammer were loud enough, two at least of Albrecht's Grail-wonders were sometimes wrought. That fantasy of the angel and dove, which came down from the vault at the moment of consecration in the Mass (16), was realized, for instance, at King's Lynn, and at Hull after the Lynn model; and Villard (plate 43) devises a similar mechanism for the reading-desk, which it is likely enough he not only planned, but executed somewhere ; when the deacon reads the Gospel, the eagle on whose wings the book reposes will turn his head to listen. Again, the vocal birds on the organ have their actual exemplars elsewhere. In vol. 18 of *Annales archéologiques* (p. 90), X. Barbier de Montault figures a drawing made by Dom Martin Gerbert, of St. Blasien, from a MS. which by its style seems German of the twelfth century. The inscription reads " Arbor fusilis de qua in Alexandri gestis legitur quod in imis inspiratur et per ora avium dulces et diversas emittit voces "— " A tree of cast metal, whereof we read in the Deeds of Alexander that it takes its breath from below, and gives forth divers sweet sounds through birds' beaks." And Barbier quotes two historical examples. The Greek emperor Theophilus (829–842) ordered two great golden organs, set with precious stones, in which the sounds came through birds ; again, one of his later successors, Constantine Porphyrogenitus (911–959) had a similar golden organ-tree with birds fixed into one side of his throne. It is quite possible that later legend attributed one of these two marvellous imperial mechanisms to the great Alexander.

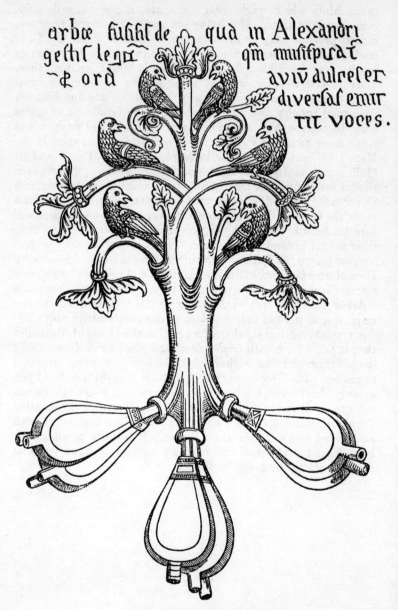

ORGAN-TREE (12TH CENTURY).

APPENDIX 32.—(Chap. XXIV, p. 473)

STANDARDIZATION BY ACT OF PARLIAMENT

STATUTE of 17 Ed. IV, Chapter 4. The King in Parliament commands : " That every such plain tile to be made shall contain in length ten inches and a half, in breadth six inches and a quarter of an inch, and in thickness half an inch and half a quarter at the least. [Roof tiles and crest-tiles to measure 13in. × ⅝in. 'with convenient deepness according'; gutter-tiles and cover-tiles to be 10½in. 'with convenient thickness, breadth and deepness according.'] And if any person or persons set to sale to any person or persons any such tile above specified, made or to be made contrary to the said ordinance, then the seller thereof shall forfeit to the buyer of the same the double value of the same tile, and besides that, shall make fine and ransom to the King at His will." Justices of the peace are to have full power of enquiry, and to inflict a fine regulated normally at 5s. per thousand bricks, 6s. 8d. for every hundred roof-tile, and 2s. per hundred corner-tile or gutter-tile, sold in contravention of this statute.

APPENDIX 33.—(CHAP. XXIV, p. 477)

MONTALEMBERT ON VANDALISM

(*Collected Works*, vol. VI, pp. 1 ff., a letter to Victor Hugo, published in the *Revue des Deux Mondes*, March 1, 1833.)

WITHIN the last few years, thanks in a great measure to Victor Hugo's own writings, " the happiest reaction has shown itself everywhere in favour of historical truth and of respect for ancient creations. France alone has remained outside and behind this movement," even behind Italy, " where the paganism of the Renaissance made most progress and struck deepest root." " In England, for more than a century, men have been restoring and building all their churches on the medieval model. . . . The King of Prussia, an intolerant Protestant sovereign, has laid upon the whole Grand Duchy of the Lower Rhine a special tax, named *Cathedral-tax*, wholly devoted to the upkeep and the gradual completion of the Catholic Cathedral of Cologne, the metropolis of Catholic art and Gothic architecture . . . . So it is only in France that vandalism reigns alone and unrestrained. After spending two centuries, and thirty years again, in dishonouring our ancient buildings with base and grotesque additions, vandalism now takes the terrorist attitude and wallows in destruction . . . . It is like a conquered land in which barbarous invaders are seeking to efface the very last traces of the generations which have dwelt in it . . . . Men cannot even respect the ruins they have themselves made." In England and Germany, owners maintain the old castles with real pride ; but, in France " the old lord puts them up for sale to the highest bidder ; the new citizen buys it . . . and both conspire together to dishonour the old stones."

In France antiquity is respected only on condition that it shall not be Christian. " You cannot melt the divans of the provinces to pity, or the *savants* of the empire, except by invoking the respect due to paganism. If you can make them believe that a church in the ante-Gothic style was dedicated to some Roman god, they will promise you protection, untie their purse-strings, and even cut their pens to honour your discovery with a dissertation.   There would be no end to the enumeration of all the Romanesque churches which are tolerated only in virtue of this ingenious creed.   I will only quote the cathedral of Angoulême, whose curious façade has been spared only because it has been gravely proved that the bas-relief of the God Almighty, which figures there among the symbols of the four evangelists, was a representation of Jupiter."

Montalembert proceeds to arrange a list of Vandals in order of merit—i.e., in proportion to their degree of hatred for "old-fashioned stuff." This list runs (p. 17): "A. *Destructive Vandals* (1) the Government, (2) Mayors and Town Councils, (3) Owners, (4) [Church] Fabric Committees and the Parish Clergy, (5) (far behind the other four) Revolt.   B. *Restoring Vandals* (1) Clergy and Fabric Committees, (2) Government, (3) Town Councils, (4) Owners.   As for Revolt, it may at least be said for it that it never restores."   After spending 23 pages on instances of destruction by the first three categories, he devotes ten more to No. 4, the Clergy (p. 44).

"They seem to have said to each other [since the Restoration of the Monarchy], 'Now the evil days will end; a new era of prosperity and brilliance will dawn for Catholicism in France; so let us put our churches in holiday trim.   We must make the poor old creatures young again; we must lend all the freshness of youth to these ancient monuments of an ancient creed; then we shall struggle better against all the new religions that swarm around us.   Up, then! let us dress them in red and blue and green and white; white above all, for that is the cheapest, and then it is the Bourbon colour too! Whitewash, scrape, paint, plaster the rouge on their faces, let us deck all this old stuff with the dazzling adornments of modern taste!   That will be as good a way as any other to prove that religion belongs to all ages and to all generations! . . . Very rarely can a parish priest resist the temptation of cheaply renovating his church, and thus marking his own administration.   He generally gives way, in spite of the opposition of the country-folk, among whom I have often found the most laudable dislike of these novelties . . . At St. Marcellin [a town in the Rhône valley] the principal church, very remarkable for its venerable age, has been adorned with an unhappy painting of the Last Judgment, in the centre of which reigns a God Almighty wearing a red wig, with the artist's signature in full, and this perfectly apposite inscription : *How terrible is this place !* " At Avignon, a chapel once used by the Popes " has been daubed with the most ludicrous paintings . . . It is doubtless to escape from the dangers of competition that this same brush has effaced the very last traces of a priceless fresco attributed to Simone Memmi of Siena, the friend of Petrarch and Laura, wherein he had painted the two lovers under the features of St. George and the maiden whom he is delivering from the dragon. The white place is still shown [to visitors]." At Beaumont there is " a new confessional, surmounted with two keys like an inn-sign, and for which I was seeking some comparison in my mind when a peasant who happened to be there hit the nail exactly : ' That looks for all the world like a booth at the fair ! ' You may imagine how much the dignity of the sacrament gains from such a comparison."

The reader will recognize here a good deal of the rhetoric, and doubtless even of the exaggerations, which make Montalembert's *Monks of the West* one of the most popular histories even to the present day. But the pertinent consideration here is that, in both these writings, he feels the inspiration of a religious champion. Addressing Victor Hugo directly again, he concludes this long article : " We, as sons of ancient Catholicism, stand here in the midst of our title-deeds of nobility ; we have the right to love them and to be proud of them   it is our duty to fight to the last for them.   That is why we call upon men in the name of ancient worship, as you call upon them in the name of art and fatherland, to repeat that cry of indignation and shame which was torn from the Popes of the great centuries by the devastation of Italy : *Let us drive these Barbarians forth !* "

APPENDIX 34.—(CHAP. XXIV, p. 478)

PUGIN'S RELIGION

From J. C. Colquhoun. *Scattered Leaves of Biography.*
London, Macintosh. 1864. Pp. 348–358.

" BUT, so far from these views being supplied to him through
Romanism, they placed him in more vehement collision
with the Romish Church and its priesthood than with the Church
he had deserted. The clergy of the Anglican Church, men of
letters and cultivation, were the first to adopt the new ideas,
and to sympathise with the restored principles of art . . . In
later days, after a longer experience, he discovered that, while
the condemned Protestant Church was purifying art, and
restoring her churches after true models, his own Church was
hopelessly given over to the vilest taste and the meanest trickery
or worship and art. The debased Italian style, to which, both
abroad and at home, the Romish ecclesiastics clung, was an
abomination which Pugin condemned with the full force of his
intrepid pen. He denounced the Romish chapels as vulgar
theatres for tawdry display. ' I once had a peep,' he says,
' into Moorfields Chapel. I saw nothing that reminded me of
the ancient religion ; from the fabric down to the vestments of
the celebrants, everything seemed strange and new ; the singing,
after the solemn chants of Westminster, sounded execrable,
and I returned perplexed and disappointed.' . . . In France
Pugin found everything execrable. In Rome he had to fly in
order to save his faith ; for the music of the Roman churches
was the music of the opera, and tripping songs were substituted
' for the song of Simeon, the hymn of St. Ambrose, and the
canticle of the Virgin.' He fared no better in the cathedral of
Cologne. . . . It is evident that, as Pugin advanced in experience
and in judgment, he became more and more dissatisfied with his
position in the Church of Rome, and conscious of the mistake
he had made in joining it. In the last work he wrote, which
he left unfinished, he traced the Reformation to one of its

undoubted causes—the vices and venality of Romish ecclesiastics
—the worldliness of the Pope and Cardinals. These evils, and
the abuses of monasteries, were described by him with a pen as
bold as Luther's ; and he shows that most of the desecration of
the buildings of that day was effected by the clergy of his own
communion. Such a man, with such independence of mind,
was a very awkward convert for the Church of Rome. They
dared not quarrel with him ; they could not renounce him—
they were compelled to humour him, and, as far as they could,
to restrain his pen. Whether they would long have been able
to do this, may be doubted. He increased in determination as
he became older. His insight into their malpractices, and his
disgust at their meanness, grew with his years. See how he
speaks of their legacy-hunting. He paints the hunting of bishops
and priests after legacies, wrung from the fears or superstitions
of the faithful, and he describes the result of this, and the indignation of the relatives of the deceased, when they found
themselves robbed and deprived of their expectations. ' The
lawyers offer their services ; it is a case for a jury ; family
interests should be protected. Proceedings are begun ; then,
to prevent scandal and to stop expense, half the property is
made over in a compromise. After this ensue rival suits between
rival bishops, and the bequest, begun in fraud, perishes in
litigation.' . . .' I should view any legal exactment, that will
induce men to be more liberal during their lives and less relying
on testamentary bequests, as a great practical blessing.' . . .
It may be taken as a proof of the extreme excitement of the brain,
which precedes the nervous system giving way, that, in addition
to his labours as an architect and to the writings upon architecture which he published, Pugin had begun, early in 1851,
a theological work. Early in that year he announced it to his
friend, Mr. Minton, and it is plain, even from the title of the
book, ' An Apology for the Church of England,' that his opinions
had undergone material change. He no longer attributed to
the Reformation the dilapidation of ecclesiastical buildings,
and the decay of taste ; and he no longer expected from the
ecclesiastics of the Romish Church the sympathy and encouragement on which he had once relied. He is reported to have said,
' The rest of my life must be one of penitence, to seek forgive-
ness for the wrong I have done to the Anglican Church.' But
we do not dwell on the hasty expressions of an excited and
diseased mind."

APPENDIX 35.—(Chap. XXV, p. 498)

VARIETIES OF CHRISTIAN SPIRIT

The Nineteenth Century and After, January 1901, p. 173 (The Right Rev. J. C. Hedley, D.D., Bishop of Newport).

" THE visibility of the Church, and the external Ministry of the sacramental system, is, as we hold, part of Christ's ordinance. And it is apparently intended for a grand moral purpose. It is intended to deepen, to regulate, and to intensify interior religion. If we believe our Lord's word, the essence of the Christian spirit is a certain childlike docility. It is a simple fact that a man cannot be childlike unless he has practised himself in submitting to another man, and in conforming himself to an external ordinance which he has not established for himself."

Ibid., February 1901, p. 306 (Herbert Paul).

" ' It is a simple fact,' says Bishop Hedley, ' that a man cannot be childlike unless he has practised himself in submitting to another man, and in conforming himself to an external ordinance which he has not established for himself.' I always distrust a man when he talks about ' simple facts.' So few facts are simple. To me this simple fact is a simple fiction refuted every day by the Society of Friends, who have the moral (not the intellectual) simplicity of children without priests or forms. They are contented with the worship of Him to whom we all pray that He will forgive us our trespasses as we forgive them that trespass against us."

INDEX OF NAMES AND PLACES

Excluding Names of Authors in the footnotes
Boldface Arabic numbers designate volume number;
Roman numerals refer to pages in Appendixes

DISCARDED

DISCARDED